X

D1211954

William Kennedy

Twayne's United States Authors Series

Frank Day, Editor

Clemson University

TUSAS 570

WILLIAM KENNEDY
Photograph © 1988 Edward C. Reilly

William Kennedy

Edward C. Reilly

Arkansas State University

Twayne Publishers
A Division of G. K. Hall & Co. • *Boston*

William Kennedy
Edward C. Reilly

Copyright 1991 by G. K. Hall & Co.
All rights reserved.
Published by Twayne Publishers
A division of G. K. Hall & Co.
70 Lincoln Street
Boston, Massachusetts 02111

Copyediting supervised by India Koopman.
Book production by Gabrielle B. McDonald.
Typeset in Garamond by Compositors Corporation of Cedar Rapids, Iowa.

First published 1991.
10 9 8 7 6 5 4 3 2 1

The paper used in this publication meets the minimum requirements
of American National Standard for Information Sciences—Permanence
of Paper for Printed Library Materials, ANSI Z39.48–1984. ∞™

Printed and bound in the United States of America.

Library of Congress Cataloging-in-Publication Data

Reilly, Edward C.
    William Kennedy / Edward C. Reilly.
        p.   cm. — (Twayne's United States authors series ; TUSAS 570)
    Includes bibliographical references and index.
    ISBN 0-8057-7611-7
    1. Kennedy, William, 1928–   —Criticism and interpretation.
    I. Title.   II. Series.
    PS3561.E428Z87   1991
    813'.54—dc20   90-44175
                                                                   CIP

In Love
for Rosemary, Bobby, Jack, Patty, Laney
and especially for my children
Heather Anne, Laurie Lynne, Erin Leigh, Jeffery Sean

Contents

Preface

Upon seeing on the cover of *Ironweed* the poignant picture of a man whose haunted, resolute face is as worn as his hat—Kennedy was also awed with this picture as he leafed through Margaret Bourke-White's *You Have Seen Their Faces*—I judged a book by its cover and was not disappointed. It was backward then to *Billy Phelan's Greatest Game, Legs, The Ink Truck,* and *O Albany!* On successive readings and analyses, these books grow more wondrous in their acute sense of place, their language, their humor, and their sense of Irishness. But Kennedy is a wondrous man who for twenty years wrote solely for the joy of writing and who has finally become recognized as a major voice in contemporary American literature.

Scholarly criticism about Kennedy's works is sparse, but three extensive interviews and numerous general newspaper and magazine articles provide insights into Kennedy's life, ideas, and writing. I augmented my research with an interview that William Kennedy graciously granted and with my own literary tour of Albany, made with the maps and information in *O Albany!*, a tour that emphasized just how closely Kennedy's plots and characters are tied to Albany. Because this is the first book-length study of William Kennedy, I concentrate on his major works—*O Albany!*, a collection of journalistic essays, and his Albany cycle novels: *The Ink Truck, Legs, Billy Phelan's Greatest Game, Ironweed,* and *Quinn's Book.* I cursorily refer to some of his published essays and to his short stories. Kennedy admits his short stories invariably turn into novels.

Kennedy emphasizes the cyclical nature of his novels. Their open-endedness permits him to weave in and out of past and present time frames in developing plot interconnections and a sense of Albany as a place. Metaphorically, each novel forms its own concentric circles that enlarge and widen until they overlap, interconnect, and complement one another's plots, themes, and characters' lives. Kennedy's personal matrix is made up of his Irish heritage, his predominantly Irish North End neighborhood in Albany, and Albany itself—with its definite place in the unfolding American panorama. Chapter 1 discusses Kennedy's Albany roots and those external forces that have not only shaped him but also influenced his writing—his parents and family, Irish-Catholicism, his predominantly Irish neighborhood, his journalistic experience, his Puerto Rican sojourn, and the movies.

Kennedy also admits that history in general fascinates him, especially the history of Albany, which he focuses on in *O Albany!* and uses again as a backdrop in his novels. In the second chapter, I analyze the *O Albany!* essays that, as Baedekers to his fiction, illuminate such essentials to his novels as the politically powerful O'Connells, John O'Connell Jr.'s kidnapping, the factual portrait of Jack "Legs" Diamond, and the description of Albany's famed Nighttown. I also analyze the *O Albany!* essays in terms of their journalistic and literary techniques, both of which become evident in his novels.

I begin my discussion of Kennedy's novels with comments from selected book reviews, some of which are insightful and others innocuously imperceptive; taken together, the reviews provide a basis for discussion. In analyzing each novel, I generally focus on characters, setting and theme, and literary structure and techniques. The concluding section of each chapter emphasizes how the novel under discussion reveals Kennedy's maturing literary style and technique and contributes to the interconnections between the novel and the works that either precede or follow it. My final chapter focuses on Kennedy's deserved place in the mainstream of American fiction.

This study is by no means exhaustive. To connect one or two plot threads, to analyze characters, to decipher one symbol, to discuss one theme, to trace a historical parallel or an allusion is to become aware of just one filigreed level—how way gives way to way, to paraphrase Robert Frost. In other words, the field for Kennedy criticism lies fallow.

Edward C. Reilly

Arkansas State University

Acknowledgments

Although acknowledgments can never go deep enough, I wish to thank Viking Penguin for permission to quote from William Kennedy's works: From *Ironweed* by William Kennedy. Copyright © 1979, 1981, 1983 by William Kennedy. All rights reserved. Reprinted by permission of Viking Penguin, Inc. From *The Ink Truck* by William Kennedy. Copyright © 1969, 1984 by William Kennedy. All rights reserved. Reprinted by permission of Viking Penguin, Inc. From *Legs* by William Kennedy. Copyright © 1975 by William Kennedy. All rights reserved. Reprinted by permission of Viking Penguin, Inc. From *O Albany!* by William Kennedy. Copyright © 1983 by William Kennedy. All rights reserved. Reprinted by permission of Viking Penguin, Inc. From *Quinn's Book* by William Kennedy. Copyright © 1988 by William Kennedy. All rights reserved. Reprinted by permission of Viking Penguin, Inc. I am also indebted to Paul Slovak for the express mail copy of *Quinn's Book,* and finally to the Liz Darhansoff Agency for permission to quote from *Billy Phelan's Greatest Game.* Copyright © 1978 by William Kennedy. All rights reserved.

Thanks also to Kay Bonetti for permission to quote from her William Kennedy interview, which I first heard through the American Audio Prose Library, a scholarly collection of taped interviews with, and in some instances, readings by contemporary authors.

I appreciate Frank Day of Clemson University and G. K. Hall's Liz Traynor, who red-inked my manuscript with insightful revisions, and I appreciate the semester leave granted by the Faculty Leave Committee of Arkansas State University.

Thanks again and again and again to Carol Sue Johnson, who typed this manuscript and numerous others, some of which I gave her in a helter-skelter panic to meet deadlines.

I also thank some of my special rainbows—Deann, Bernee, Deborah Jane, Cheryl, and especially Cathy Ivey (aka Rags).

For the interview, the letters, the advice, the offer to read my manuscript for any "gremlins" therein, for expediting the advanced copy of *Quinn's Book,* and especially for writing those enjoyable, wondrous, and enduring works of his, I say to Bill Kennedy, "May God hold you in the palm of his hand."

Chronology

1928   William Joseph Kennedy born 16 January in North Albany to William Joseph, Sr., and Mary Elizabeth McDonald Kennedy.

1933   Enrolls in Public School 20 in North Albany.

1941–1945   Attends Christian Brothers Academy and writes for the *Sentry,* the school newspaper.

1945–1949   Attends Siena College, Loudonville, New York; earns B.A. degree; edits *Siena News* and is an associate editor of the *Beverwyck,* both college publications.

1950   Becomes sportswriter and columnist for the *Post Star,* Glens Falls, New York; drafted into the U.S. Army, serves in Europe as sports editor for *Ivy Leaves,* the Fourth Division's newspaper.

1956   Moves to San Juan, Puerto Rico, to become a columnist and assistant managing editor of the *Puerto Rico World Journal* (San Juan).

1957   Marries Ana Daisy (Dana) Segarra; reporter for *Miami* [Florida] *Herald*; correspondent for Time-Life publications and reporter for *Dorvillier* (business) *Newsletter* and Knight Newspapers.

1958   Dana Elizabeth born 7 January.

1959   Becomes founding managing editor of the *San Juan Star*; Katherine Anne born 4 June.

1960   Enrolls in Saul Bellow's creative writing workshop, University of Puerto Rico, Rio Piedras, Puerto Rico.

1961   Resigns as *San Juan Star* managing editor to write fiction full time.

1963   Returns to Albany to continue as a full-time novelist; part-time journalist for *Albany Times Union*; begins newspaper series about Albany's neighborhoods and ethnic groups; strike at *Times Union* becomes basis for a short story.

1964   Completes a newspaper series that becomes the basis for *0 Albany!*

1965   Nominated for a Pulitzer Prize for his Albany slum articles; NAACP Award for reporting.

1968   Film critic for *Albany Times Union,* a position held until 1970.

1969   *The Ink Truck.*

1970   Brendan Christopher born 3 July.

1971   Book editor for *Look Magazine.*

1973   *Letter to a Would-Be Journalist, IV,* and *Letter to a Would-Be Writer—Fiction, II* (course modules).

1974   Part-time lecturer, State University of New York at Albany, a position held until 1982.

1975   *Legs.*

1978   *Billy Phelan's Greatest Game.*

1980   Honorary L.H.D., Russell Sage College, Troy, New York.

1982   Visiting professor, Cornell University, Ithaca, New York.

1983   *Ironweed, 0 Albany!, Legs,* and *Billy Phelan's Greatest Game* reissued; *The Cotton Club* script completed. Receives MacArthur Foundation Fellowship and National Book Critics Circle Award for *Ironweed;* named PEN-Faulkner Award finalist. Establishes Writers Institute at Albany. Receives tenure and full professorship, State University of New York at Albany.

1984   Receives Pulitzer Prize for Fiction for *Ironweed;* Casey Michael Rafferty, grandson, born on same day Pulitzer is announced. Receives New York State's Governor's Art Award; Frank O'Connor Literary Award; Columbus Foundation Award for *0 Albany!;* and honorary L.H.D., Siena College. Governor Mario Cuomo and the state legislature make the Writers Institute a state-supported establishment; Albany declares "A City-Wide Celebration of Albany and William Kennedy" (6–9 September). *The Cotton Club* premieres in Albany and New York City.

1985   Honorary L.H.D., College of St. Rose, Albany, New York.

1986   *Charley Malarkey and the Belly Button Machine,* coauthored by Brendan Kennedy. Creative Arts Award Citation, Brandeis University, Waltham, Massachusetts.

1987 *Ironweed,* the film, premieres in Albany.

1988 *Quinn's Book.*

Chapter One
"For the Life of the Soul": Albany Roots and Other Fortuities

A Northender

In "Albany as a State of Mind," the first essay in *O Albany!*, William Kennedy identifies his Albany ties: "I write this book not as a booster of Albany, which I am, nor as an apologist for the city, which I sometimes am, but rather as a person whose imagination has become fused with a single place, and in that place, finds all the elements that a man needs for the life of the soul."[1] After terming Albany a "magical place where the past becomes visible if one is willing to track the multiple incarnations of the city's soul," Kennedy concludes by declaring his literary purpose: "It is the task of this and other books I have written, and hope to write, to peer into the heart of this always-shifting past, to be there when it ceases to be what it was, when it becomes what it must under scrutiny, when it turns so magically, so inevitably, from then into now" (*OA*, 7). These statements emphasize Kennedy's strong Albany roots and ties, and provide insights into his fictional world—its plots, characters, and themes. To understand the biographical details that shaped Kennedy's being and ideas is to understand and appreciate his fiction.

In January 1928, William Joseph Kennedy was born to William Joseph, Sr., and Mary Elizabeth McDonald Kennedy, whose Irish ancestors had settled in Albany several generations before. This Irish–Catholic heritage figures prominently in Kennedy's life and fiction. Kennedy grew up on North Pearl Street in Albany's predominantly Irish–Catholic North End, or, as it was often called, Limerick. As a Northender, Kennedy attended Mass at Sacred Heart Church where he was also an altar boy. He went to grade school at Public School 20, high school at Christian Brothers Academy, and graduated with a Bachelor of Arts degree from Siena College—a Franciscan school in Loudonville, New York. As did a number of his friends and classmates, Kennedy aspired to the priesthood—"for wasn't the cloth the grandest thing a young man could wear?"—but, he adds, "not be-

yond the seventh grade, for even by then I intuited my embrace of the pro-
fane: I was drawing cartoons, printing my own newspaper, fixated on the
world of print" (*OA, 25*).

Regarding his Irish–Catholic heritage, Kennedy admits that he tried to
resist it all by walking out of Mass "during narrowback sermons" and by
refusing to sing "Too-ra-loo-ra-loo-ra" only to realize: "I thought myself free,
and found out that not only wasn't I free, I was fettered to all of it, most
surprisingly the Irishness, which was the only element of my history that
wasn't organized, the only one I couldn't resign from, and, further, the only
one that hadn't been shoved down my throat" (*OA, 39*). In fact, Gerald
Howard, an Irish Catholic and Kennedy's Viking editor, claims that
Kennedy's "Irishness is a real key to who he is and what he is thinking."[2] In
recalling his formative years in North Albany, which Kennedy terms a "Crucible for Childhood," the title of one *O Albany!* essay, he says, "The North
End made me and nothing exists powerful enough to unmake me without
destroying the vessel" (*OA, 40*).

Regarding Catholicism and its influences on his life and fiction, Kennedy
claims that the "formalities of the Catholic Church" do not interest him and
that religions interest him "only to the extent that they suggest something at
the heart of everyone's lives. I believe in the mystical relationships that exist
among things."[3] In discussing *Ironweed,* however, Kennedy refers to Francis
Phelan's Dantean "journey through planes of escalation into a moment of redemption out of sin" and then emphasizes the North End and Catholic
matrix:

Francis cleanses himself. It reflects something profound about human behavior. I
don't look at it in the way that I used to when I was a kid, when I believed in everything, believed it was the only way to look at the world. Today I believe Catholic the-
ology has great humanistic dimensions, a great wisdom about how to achieve peace
of mind in relationship to the unknown, the infinite. Maybe it's a palliative. Maybe
it's one of the great lollipops of history. At the same time it's beautiful. It's as good as
I could see on the horizon. I don't need Buddhism, or Zoroastrianism—I've got the
Sacred Heart Church in North Albany.[4]

As a Northender, Kennedy was also influenced in his life and his writings
by Irish–Democratic politics. His great-grandfather, Big Jim Carroll, had
been an influential political leader of North Albany's Ninth Ward, and
Carroll's son, John, and his grandson, Jim, Kennedy's great-uncle and uncle,
were ward politicians. After working as a barber and as a foundry laborer,
Kennedy's father, William Sr., became Albany County's deputy sheriff. He

always worked at the polls and took young Kennedy to political rallies. On his mother's side of the family was a similar story. Her uncles Coop and Jim McDonald held political appointments, and says Kennedy, "I can think of half a dozen more family ties to the city or county payrolls." (*OA*, 45). Kennedy emphasizes that the major political force in Albany and in his life was Daniel Peter O'Connell. One of the nation's longest-running political machines began with O'Connell's election as the county assessor in 1919 and continued long after his death in 1977. The O'Connell Democratic machine, which controlled both city and county politics, had become such a legacy that James McGregor Burns thought it should be preserved in the "Smithsonian before we forget what a political machine looks like" (*OA*, 45). Regarding the O'Connell influence, Kennedy writes:

> Your identity was fixed by both religion and politics, but from the political hierarchy came the way of life; the job, the perpetuation of the job, the dole when there was no job, the loan when there was no dole, the security of the neighborhood, . . . the right to run your bar after hours or to open a card game on the sneak. These things came to you not by right of citizenship. Republicans had no such rights. They came to you because you gave allegiance to Dan O'Connell and his party. The power he held was so pervasive that you often didn't even know it existed until you contravened it. Then God help you, poor soul. Cast into outer darkness. (*OA*, 43–44)

In *Billy Phelan's Greatest Game*, Kennedy uses the O'Connell machine as the model for the McCalls' political machine and its pervasive power that can close Albany's Nighttown world to Billy Phelan because he refused to cooperate with the McCalls.

In "Legacy from a Lady" in *O Albany!*, Kennedy recalls how at age ten he discovered the magic of books in the John Van Schaick Lansing Pruyn Library branch on North Pearl Street where he read "good books." "The trashy ones," he adds, "I collected on my own, stored them in the attic, and entered their *magic* with the firm intuition from my uncle that trash is also good for the soul" (*OA*, 8). For Kennedy, the beauty and magic of books included those by Charles Dickens, Jack London, Nordoff and Hall, Rafael Sabatini, and O. Henry, and stories about Tom Swift and Sherlock Holmes. One of the most influential authors for Kennedy was John Steinbeck, whom Kennedy first thought of as "that most loathsome purveyor of scandalous language." In *Of Mice and Men*, Kennedy had read "no more than six pages before I came across a g——d d———n and even more blasphemous utterances, right there on the printed page" (*OA*, 10). Shocked because of his Catholic upbringing, Kennedy returned the novel to the library only to check it out later, read it, and find himself "weeping for Lennie, weeping even more vigorously for George," and becoming a "Steinbeck freak for years to come" (*OA*, 10).

After reading Steinbeck, Kennedy vowed that no person or institution would ever "hold censoring power" over what he read, so he read "Joyce and Lawrence, Miller and Mailer, *Penthouse* and *Screw*" (*OA*, 10). As evidenced by the epigraphs to his novels, Kennedy has read Dante (*Ironweed*); Johan Huizinga and Carl Jung (*Billy Phelan's Greatest Game*); Eugene Ionesco (*Legs*); Robert Benchley, Victor Appleton, Don Marquis, Joseph Campbell, William Butler Yeats, and William Saroyan (*The Ink Truck*); Albert Camus and Leonardo da Vinci (*Quinn's Book*). In talking about literature, Kennedy often alludes to Milan Kundera, Günter Grass, Gabriel García Márquez (Kennedy's personal friend), and to Ernest Hemingway, William Faulkner, and John Cheever. In addition, Kennedy also wrote book reviews for *Life, Look*, the *National Observer*, the *New Republic, New York Times, Saturday Review*, and *Washington Post*. According to Kennedy, writers are the "products of their own imagination, of their own experiences—and of other writers."[5] Although claiming he is not a book collector, Kennedy describes his Averill Park home library and its "life's worth of treasured books":

It's got everything . . . I have books since I was a kid. An enormous amount of fiction—that's the dominant thing. Lots of books from Latin America and a fairly decent film and theater library. A lot of Irish literature. Then the religion books, philosophy, psychology, politics. There's some Dante, Joseph Campbell—*The Masks of God*, a monumental work. Myths, Celtic literature. The books spill out into the hallway . . . I have some complete sets—Hemingway, Joyce, most of Faulkner . . . The history of the city, almanacs, peculiar memoirs. Historical picture books, curiosities, histories of churches and schools, peculiar stuff.[6]

Kennedy also acknowledges the influences that both his father and his uncle Pete McDonald had on him. They introduced him to Albany's male world of pool shooting, gambling, and bowling, pastimes he pursued at the Knights of Columbus hall at 131 North Pearl Street. Later he bowled in the Simmons Machine Tool Corporation Bowling League. Kennedy's father was also a skilled bowler who during one match made the rare "double-pinochle split (4–6–7–10) pins."[7] Regarding his father's more pervasive influence, Kennedy says, "I keep hearing phrases, representing values that were his, which he never really tried to impose on me but did in the same way that the church and the Democratic Party and the North End of Albany did—that matrix."[8]

Kennedy describes Pete McDonald, his avowed favorite uncle, as a "wild man . . . who did many basic things well: bowling, talking, shooting pool, or darts" and who could cover a dart board with a newspaper, have someone call out a number, hit it, then call out another number, and hit it also ("Fast Lane," 60). Once Pete bowled a 299 game and chided young Kennedy, "When you roll 300, come around and talk to me"; ten years later Kennedy bowled 299 and "therewith shut Pete up about the 300" ("Fast Lane," 60). Years later in Puerto Rico while Kennedy searched for his fictional corner of the universe about which to write, he admitted that the "shape of the ball returns in the Knights of Columbus alleys . . . were artifacts out of a significant past—my father's, my uncle's, my own" (*OA*, 4). These artifacts emerge in *Billy Phelan's Greatest Game*—Billy bowls 299, and his characterization is based on Pete McDonald: "Pete . . . was very important to me . . . He had a special quality in his attitude toward life, which was one of great vivacity. He had a great sense of humor and absolutely original attitudes. He was a magical character. He personified the age. He's one of the prototypes of Billy Phelan."[9]

Stop the Presses

Kennedy's interest in journalism and in being a newspaperman also figures prominently in his life and in his fiction. Sometime about the seventh grade he became interested in the world of print and wrote his own newspaper. He worked on his high school's paper, read several daily papers, and dreamed of becoming a columnist. After graduating from Siena College, where he had been the executive editor for the *Siena News* (later named the *Indian*), he was a columnist and sports editor for the *Post Star* in Glens Falls, New York. Drafted into the Army in 1950 during the Korean Conflict, he served in Europe as the sports editor for the Fourth Division's newspaper— Hemingway's World War II division—and recalls, "They gave me a jeep, and I ran around Europe covering ball games and golf tournaments and the Olympics and had a great time."[10]

After his discharge in 1952, Kennedy returned to Albany and worked for the *Times Union* until 1956 when he eagerly accepted a job as a columnist and assistant managing editor for the *Puerto Rico World Journal*, a paper for English-speaking inhabitants of Puerto Rico; it became defunct after only nine months. After moving to Miami and reporting for the *Miami Herald* for less than a year, Kennedy returned to Puerto Rico, and in 1959 became the founding managing editor of the *San Juan Star*. In 1963 he returned permanently to Albany to care for his ailing father; he worked part-time for the

Times Union because he did not want newspaper work to interfere with his fiction writing. During his stint, the *Times Union*'s management and employees became embroiled in a strike which would provide the inspiration for *The Ink Truck*, Kennedy's first novel. During 1963 and 1964, Kennedy wrote a series of twenty-six articles about Albany's history, politics, leaders, and neighborhoods. In 1982 these articles became the basis for *O Albany!*, but only after new reporting and total rewriting because, to quote Kennedy, "the prose was dead. Also, I realized the neighborhoods had changed drastically in 17 years—some weren't even there anymore. So I had to do a lot of new reporting."[11] In 1965, Kennedy was nominated for the Pulitzer Prize for Journalism for a series he wrote about Albany's slums, a series which rankled Dan O'Connell and his political machine. To quote his fellow journalist John McLoughlin, "Kennedy's series on poverty in Albany was a daring thing to do at the time . . . It was an affront to the Machine. Those articles really caused a stir."[12]

Kennedy's dedication and verve in reporting also earned him praise, and William J. Dorvillier, one of Kennedy's editors, says he was "a hell of a newspaperman" and "one of the best complete journalists—as reporter, editor, whatever—that I've known in sixty years in the business."[13] Kennedy says his reporting style is "to saturate myself with information . . . When I wrote a series on slum housing in Albany for the *Times Union,* I reported on it for three months before I began to write."[14] As a newspaperman, Kennedy thought he might never be a successful fiction writer but rather a "kind of O. Henry or a Runyon or a Mark Twain at his most casual," but in 1952 he began to write short stories that made some sense."[15] He adds, however, "I wrote a lot of stories that didn't go anywhere, and after a while I gave up. I was working from a distant outsider's perch looking longingly at the literary culture without being able to enter it. And then I just decided to hell with it. I'll just go for the novel."[16]

While admitting that journalism is a "great training ground" and that "no bailbondsman, no lawyer, no politician, no bartender, no actor can enter into the variety of worlds that a journalist can," Kennedy believes that his life's purpose is to write fiction and declares that "writing novels is what I'm supposed to do in this world"; furthermore, he realizes that despite the marvelous journalistic techniques of James Agee, Gay Talese, and Tom Wolfe, "the great novels give you things no journalist can give you."[17] He stresses the novel's "freedom to bring in the unknown. In creating a human being, a character, you take off from the complexity of life."[18] Before writing *Legs,* for example, he saturated himself with research about Diamond's life and career only to learn that he eventually had to reinvent Diamond as a literary character. In another instance, he wrote articles about skid row bums for the *Times Union* and wanted to publish these as *The Lemon Weed*—first as non-fiction, then as a novella—but he discovered that "nobody wanted to publish a book about a bunch of bums talking to each other."[19] After setting *The Lemon Weed* aside and writing *Billy Phelan's Greatest Game*, Kennedy translated some details from *The Lemon Weed* into the more mature fiction of *Ironweed*.

Within journalistic realms, Kennedy is another of the many journalists who have turned to fiction: Walt Whitman, Mark Twain, Stephen Crane, Jack London, Frank Norris, James T. Farrell, Willa Cather, John Dos Passos, Ernest Hemingway, and John Hersey. While the new journalists (Joan Didion, Hunter S. Thompson, George Plimpton) and nonfiction novels (Tom Wolfe's *The Electric Kool-Aid Acid Test*, Truman Capote's *In Cold Blood*, Norman Mailer's *The Executioner's Song*) have blurred the "line between fact and fiction,"[20] many journalists, Kennedy included, feel that journalism can never accomplish what fiction can, and so they inevitably turn to fiction. Kennedy's journalism sharpened his eye for specific and accurate details, nurtured his love of words, and helped develop his sense for the dramatic leads that open his narratives.

A Puerto Rican Tourist

From Kennedy's sojourn in Puerto Rico emerged several biographical details that have shaped his life and his fiction. First, he married Ana Daisy (Dana) Segarra, a former model (her picture graced the cover of *Look* magazine, 17 January 1961) and Broadway dancer (her stage name was Dana Sosa). She has supported his desire to write fiction: "I knew that Bill had to keep writing . . . no matter what. I understood his artistic drives because I remembered my own when I was a young dancer. I knew he had to live with his passion to write, and I had to live with it, too, or I wouldn't have a marriage."[21] Recalling his struggling years as a writer, Kennedy readily praises Dana for her moral support and faith in him: "It is also essential to acknowledge the gift my wife, Dana, has for keeping me as happy as any writer can ever expect to be, and who is very good at putting together superior children, which she has done three times without losing her talent for making unbearably good cognac chicken and running a business and teaching dance and managing our precarious finances in a way that kept us out of the debtor's prison" (*OA*, 378–79).

His own family ties have helped nurture close bonds between Kennedy and his three children, Dana Elizabeth, Katherine Anne, and Brendan

Christopher. In acknowledging these ties, Kennedy dedicates *The Ink Truck* to Dana and his daughters, "the three elegant ladies I live with," and *Billy Phelan's Greatest Game* to Brendan, "a nifty kid," with whom Kennedy co-authored *Charley Malarkey and the Belly Button Machine,* a book for children, set in Albany, and dedicated to Kennedy's grandchildren, "Casey and Shannon Rafferty, two new kids on the block, of whom the authors are, respectively, new uncle and not-so-new grandfather."[22] In the "Authors' Note," Kennedy and Brendan vow that each wrote "exactly fifty percent" of *Charley Malarkey,* the plot of which evolved when four-year-old Brendan would go to bed, his pajamas would ride up exposing his belly button, and Kennedy and Brendan would concoct stories about the belly button, stories which they polished and refined through the years.

Second, in 1960 Kennedy enrolled in a creative writing course taught by Saul Bellow, then a visiting professor at the University of Puerto Rico at Rio Piedras. Not only was Bellow "very, very encouraging," say Kennedy, "but he confirmed my belief that I had something to say."[23] Later, when *Ironweed* had been rejected by Viking and thirteen other publishers—among these were Dial; Knopf; Holt, Rinehart, & Winston; Houghton Mifflin; Random House—Bellow advised Viking's Corlies "Cork" Smith:

I've just read Wm. Kennedy's *Billy Phelan*—a real novel, for a change. Enough to make you believe that under the masses of published garbage literature still lives. You were his editor, I don't need to win you to my opinion. But why has Viking stopped publishing him? The company is making a serious mistake. These Albany novels will be memorable, a distinguished group of books, and they ought to be done by a single publisher. They aren't making any money now, but they eventually will make a great deal of it. Kennedy is the sort of writer Viking should invest in . . . I'd be willing to help out. That the author of *Billy* should have a manuscript kicking around, looking for a publisher is disgraceful.[24]

Despite his claim that someone would have inevitably recognized Kennedy's literary talents, Bellow's letter proved significant. Cork Smith bought *Ironweed* as an unfinished book, but then left publishing for personal reasons. Kennedy disagreed with the editors who succeeded Smith and parted company with Viking. When Bellow wrote the letter, however, Smith had returned to Viking. "Now there was a big difference," Smith said. "Of course, it was the same book . . . But now it had been kissed by a Nobel Prize winner. I also knew that Saul did not do this casually; he doesn't puff things. Nobody takes a Bellow quote casually. So with a Nobel Prize winner in my pocket, and with Bellow's offer to help, I thought 'Let's take a chance.' "[25] In

Kennedy's case, Bellow had no need to "puff things" because in 1960 he had recognized Kennedy's talents:

> He could take material from skid row and write about these people as fully human as anyone else. The people he wrote about didn't know they had become pariahs. He wrote about them from the inside. And it was very touching. I was moved by the characters, by their naive but human frailties.
>
> Kennedy's books show some very original insights . . . His treatment of the characters is very far from the usual hackneyed treatment. There are no dead sentences in his work. He's just very gifted. At a time when so much cold porridge is served up in the literary world as hot stuff, here is real hot stuff. In his books nothing is being put over on the public. He doesn't latch on to subjects so that the book can be sold. He's just a pure writer.[26]

Finally, Kennedy realized how strong his ties to Albany were, the city he thought he had escaped from when he eagerly accepted the position at the *Puerto Rico World Journal*. Once in Puerto Rico, however, Kennedy constantly pored over the "pages of a picture book of Albany scenes from 1867 and 1842 and 1899, trying to understand my life from these photos instead of from the bright, seaspun life around me" (*OA*, 4). He even tried to write stories about Puerto Rico, but they were shallow because he felt like a "tourist" who neither knew nor felt anything about Puerto Rico; consequently, he decided "to hell with it," began writing about Albany and says the "transition was extraordinary. I found myself ranging through sixty years of the history of the family, the Phelan family . . . I found that by focusing on these people and locations something happened to my imagination that freed me to invent readily . . . It became magical."[27]

When he returned to Albany to care for his ailing father, Kennedy began searching for answers about his heritage and about who he was. When he wrote his series of Albany articles in 1963 and 1964, he knew Albany would be his fictional world: "It was these years that my mind changed on Albany, that I came to see it as an inexhaustible context for the stories I had planned to write, as abundant in mythic qualities as it was in political ambition, remarkably consequential greed, and genuine fear of the Lord" (*OA*, 5). Kennedy crystallizes his before-and-after attitudes toward Albany in an epigraph to *O Albany!*: "This book is dedicated to people who used to think they hated the place where they grew up, and then took a second look." Retrospectively, Kennedy writes that his Puerto Rican years were a "young writer's education in discovering his own turf."[28]

His Own Turf

Kennedy says that the literature he cares "most about comes out of a deeply rooted sense of place" and without which "the work is reduced to a cry of voices in empty rooms, a literature of the self; at its best poetic music; at its worst, a thin gruel of the ego."[29] Later he comments that place is "one of the principal ingredients in fiction" because "we are what we are because of place to some degree. We interact with it (and) with its mores,"[30] an idea echoing his statement that Albany's North End has been his personal crucible. Kennedy's Albany becomes, therefore, his fictional corner of the world, where all of his novels take place (including *Legs,* despite its secondary settings in New York City, the Catskills, and Europe).

In addition, with its male protagonists, Kennedy's fictional world is a man's world—the newspaper world in *The Ink Truck,* the gangster world in *Legs,* Albany's Nighttown world in *Billy Phelan's Greatest Game,* the world of bums in *Ironweed,* and the world of war, gambling, show business, and sports in *Quinn's Book.* The male-orientation of Kennedy's worlds results in part from his associations with his father and his uncle Pete McDonald and in part from the times about which Kennedy writes, the 1840s, 1860s, 1920s, and 1930s. In refuting a critic who faulted him about not treating women seriously in *Billy Phelan's Greatest Game,* Kennedy replies, "That's ridiculous criticism because that book was a book about money, about a society of males. You didn't *see* women in that society . . . tables for ladies, back entrance, that's the way it was."[31] Although *Quinn's Book* is primarily set in a male world, Magdalena Colon and Maud Fallon, exotic dancers and performers, are part of this world, but Kennedy emphasizes that women who interacted with this male world were "on the fringe of the show business element, or . . . ladies of the evening."[32]

The North Pearl Street Knights of Columbus, a Catholic men's fraternal organization that Kennedy joined when he was seventeen, definitely influenced his fictional male world. In "My Life in the Fast Lane," an article appearing in an *Esquire* issue devoted to "The American Male: 1946–1986" and appropriately subtitled "Growing Up Male: The Way It Was," Kennedy describes the K of C as a place where "women came . . . only for parties, dances, and bingo; club life excluded them otherwise"; Kennedy also recalls that some members either sent their female companions to the movies across the street while the men socialized, or if they had dates, the men took the women home first and then went to the K of C "where life went on until perhaps midnight, adjourning finally to the Grand Lunch across the street for 'coffee and' " ("Fast Lane," 60).

It's Show Time

Another biographical detail figuring prominently in Kennedy's life and fiction is the movies. He recalls that as a young boy it was customary to go to the movies on weekends, and he "saw everything"—the Shadow serials at the Grand, the Green Arrow serials at the Ritz; and the newly constructed Palace: "When I was a kid it was awesome with all the marble."[33] However, when he saw the foreign films of Ingmar Bergman, Federico Fellini, and Luis Bunuel, to name a few, his ideas about movies changed and he realized that they were a serious art form. Kennedy was a film critic for the *Times Union* in 1963, and after a leave of absence to write *The Ink Truck,* he reviewed films during the New York Film Festival. "And God, it was stunning! An immersion in movies. I'd see five a day. That was in '68 or '69."[34] Kennedy admits that he had wanted to write screenplays ever since he was young and that when he experienced his financially difficult years, he desperately tried to write a screenplay. Kennedy's opportunity to participate in films finally came when Francis Ford Coppola asked him to screenwrite *The Cotton Club,* and although he was financially stable by then, Kennedy quickly agreed because, as he said, "It's a world that gives me pleasure."[35]

According to the screen credits, the movie was suggested by Jim Haskins's *The Cotton Club,* a pictorial history of the famous Harlem supper club from 1920 to its more uptown to Broadway when eventually, on 10 June 1940, it closed its doors forever. When former heavyweight Jack Johnson opened the club it was the Club Deluxe, but the Club Deluxe was not successful until mobster Owen "Owney" Madden bought out Johnson—Madden wanted an East Coast outlet for his "Madden's No. 1" beer. Johnson was retained in a token managerial position and Madden changed the club's name to the Cotton Club. With Madden in full control (but listed as only a minor officer), Sam Sellis as titular president, George "Big Frenchy" DeMange as secretary, and former machine gunner Herman Stark as stage manager, the Cotton Club flourished. Madden's syndicate increased the club's seating capacity, inaugurated a "whites only" policy, hired only "high yaller" chorus girls—"nothing darker than a light olive tint"—and "high-stepping, gyrating, snake-dancing" male performers, and ensured that the food, drinks, and service were always uptown and sophisticated. Not only did the Cotton Club attract a famous white clientele that included Jimmy Durante, Irving Berlin, Babe Ruth, Milton Berle, Eddie Duchin, and Ray Bolger, it also fostered the careers of such notable black entertainers as Duke Ellington, Cab Calloway, Louis "Satchmo"

Armstrong, Ethel Waters, Lena Horne, Dorothy Dandridge, Ivy Anderson, and the Nicholas Brothers.

The Cotton Club movie begins in 1928 and ends in 1931, the club's most dynamic years, and years with which Kennedy was familiar, in general, from researching and writing his novels and O Albany! essays. Kennedy admits that although he knew nothing about the Cotton Club, he had a "sense of the era and so it was a matter of finding out what was usable from it."[36] Kennedy also said that he had read Haskins's book and that he and Coppola had talked to hundreds of performers and people who had been either directly or indirectly connected with the club.[37] The film traces a number of interconnected plots and characters, all of which are developed with the Harlem nightspot as a backdrop and a symbol of the times, or, as Haskins prefaces his history: "This is not a story of Harlem. It is not, really, a story of black people. It is the story of a peculiar institution called the Cotton Club, of the world in which it flourished and of the people who made it famous."[38] Regarding the film's interconnections and nuances, Kennedy says, "The film is a version of a kind of modern short story where what's suggested is important and what's delineated is very little. A Raymond Carver story, or the early Hemingway stuff. Even The Old Man and the Sea, where he articulated the iceberg principle; one-eighth above the water and the other seven-eighths suggested."[39]

Kennedy admits that he and Coppola wrote between "forty and fifty drafts" and that much of the material "found its way on to the writing room floor," but he would not "second guess" Coppola's editing.[40] Although he admits that this screenwriting is the "most bizarre piece of writing" he has ever done, he emphasizes that he and Coppola "created the story of Dixie Dwyer."[41] Still, The Cotton Club employs some of Kennedy's literary techniques: the interconnections between characters' lives, the merging of fact and fiction, and especially the dialogue that Coppola ordered the performers to follow exactly because it worked "dramatically."[42] According to Richard T. Jameson:

Oddly enough . . . The Cotton Club may be literary rather than cinematic. Kennedy wrote the screenplay with Coppola . . . and I suspect that besides contributing some fine, tough dialogue, he inspired in Coppola a sense of narrative rigor that the director's post-Godfather films have crucially lacked. Kennedy's "Albany novels" . . . move to a rhythm of pungent detail and suggested elision that is achieved in the movement of this film—terse and jazzy rather than slow and operatic in the manner of the Godfather.[43]

Homo Mirabilis, Annus Mirabilis

Before *Ironweed*'s phenomenal success, Kennedy told Kay Bonetti, director of American Audio Prose Library, that during his writing career he had "fun along the way," was not "denied any taste of success, but it was just a taste."[44] After publishing *The Ink Truck,* he had no trouble publishing *Legs,* which became a Book-of-the-Month Club alternate selection, received over a hundred favorable reviews, became a film option, and sold sixty-five hundred copies. Despite favorable reviews, *Billy Phelan's Greatest Game* sold only thirty-five hundred copies, and, admits Kennedy, did not "make a nickel." Thus began Kennedy's dark publishing years: "*Billy Phelan* was badly publicized and cheaply publicized too. It was scandalous the way they treated that book. I was an absolute innocent and let it all happen. They treated it like a Mafia book, as if that were the way to go."[45] Even Cork Smith admits that *Billy Phelan* was "published badly."[46]

While the manuscript's odyssey may be one of the publishing world's ironies and legends, *Ironweed* would eventually become Kennedy's metaphorical nemesis and his leprechaun's gold. In a letter (29 April 1988), Kennedy writes that a "number of mistakes that the press has made through the years are being perpetuated" regarding his "separation from Viking," and he wants to correct them whenever possible.[47] After Viking editor Cork Smith bought *Ironweed* for $12,500 and Kennedy received "some money when they bought it," Smith left Viking; and, says Kennedy, the "novel moved into the hands of other editors who did not value it as much as Cork had. They were quite cool, but were going to publish it even so, yet not with the same sort of splash that Cork had in mind" (Letter, 29 April 1988). Viking then assigned Kennedy's manuscript to an editor who lived in Georgia and came to New York every two months. Kennedy writes: "This was a woman who had been very well thought of in New York, and had she been on the staff I would have been quite happy, but I disliked intensely the idea of having an editor so far removed from New York, especially when I could not count on too many friendly faces in other editorial quarters of the house" (Letter, 29 April 1988). When Kennedy called her and apologized for being unable to accept such a "remote editor," she understood his position and even wrote him a "very pleasant and understanding reply" (Letter, 29 April 1988). Kennedy admits, however, "This got Viking's nose very much out of joint. There were words between my agent and some editor at Viking with the upshot being that we separated and I took the book to sell elsewhere. This I believe was a very big relief for the Viking editors and for a moment it looked to me like a very good beginning" (Letter, 29 April 1988).

Henry Robbins, an E.P. Dutton editor, looked forward to receiving the *Ironweed* manuscript and adding Kennedy to the "Dutton list," but while the book was on Robbins' desk, Robbins "dropped dead in a New York subway on the way to work," and reports Kennedy:

That began the very weird odyssey of the manuscript through thirteen rejections. I changed agents in this period and went over to Liz Darhansoff. Liz saw fit to try Viking again because Cork Smith had returned to his editing post. Cork apparently was either powerless to accept *Ironweed* again or merely reluctant in the face of hostility to the book, and to me, that was prevalent at Viking.

The book bounced around to every large house in New York and I accumulated the rejection slips with great wonderment. One major editor told me "Nobody has ever written better on this subject matter, but I just can't publish another novel that won't make any money." It was in this bleak period of my life that I got an assignment from *Esquire* to interview Bellow. When I went to Vermont, he had just read *Billy Phelan* for the first time and it was on the basis of reading this book and not *Ironweed* that he wrote the letter to Cork Smith that changed my world. (Letter, 29 April 1988)

On Bellow's recommendation, Viking published *Ironweed,* and unlike *Billy Phelan, Ironweed* was publicized and published well mainly because of Victoria Myers, a Viking publicity director.[48] Moreover, Viking reissued Kennedy's other novels, and William Kennedy gained the critical recognition he enjoys today.

In two years, *Ironweed* sold more than one hundred thousand copies, and it has been published, along with *Legs* and *Billy Phelan,* in France, Germany, Greece, Finland, Yugoslavia, Denmark, Brazil, Spain, and Italy. Kennedy also won the Pulitzer Prize and the National Book Critics Circle Award for *Ironweed.* Kennedy attributes *Ironweed*'s success and his other novels' rediscovery not only to Bellow's influential letter but also to their cyclic interconnections: "I think that it is the concentration of books about a single place with interconnected characters, and people recognizing now that there is a cycle here, which is how I see it and what I've been calling it for years . . . It was something that I came to early on because I knew I could write about Albany at great length and not exhaust the subject matter."[49] In explaining the theory of his Albany *cycle* novels, Kennedy writes:

I had been thinking about all my books being interconnected and had arrived at the word "cycle" because it was open-ended. It would never be just a trilogy, or a septology or any particular number until I was finished writing forever. The notion that the cycle was a publishing gimmick is not true, and it wasn't Viking's invention. But it was that sort of idea that Cork originally had in mind when he first bought the book [*Ironweed*]—to emphasize the interconnectedness of my works. (Letter, 29 April 1988)

Moreover, on his birthday in 1983, Kennedy unexpectedly received a $264,000 grant from the John D. and Catherine T. MacArthur Foundation, after which, quotes Dana, Kennedy walked around the house repeating, "How sweet it is!"[50] Besides coauthoring *The Cotton Club* screenplay, Kennedy sold the screen rights to *Legs, Billy Phelan's Greatest Game,* and *Ironweed.* The last premiered at Albany's Palace Theater in December 1987. Kennedy says that *Legs* and *Billy Phelan* are both "very possible for film . . . and I will write the screenplay for them, possibly even produce the films and in a certain way become a producer."[51] In "Having the Time of His Life," Peter S. Prescott and Susan Angrest appropriately label 1983 as Kennedy's "personal *annus mirabilis* (wondrous year),"[52] an idea echoed by a friend who called Kennedy a "*homo mirabilis* (wondrous man)."[53]

Indeed, 1983 had been a wondrous and miraculous year for Kennedy, especially after considering the long years during which he wrote solely for the joy of writing. Tom Smith, one of the "four good men" to whom Kennedy dedicates *Ironweed,* says of those bleak years:

This was a man who felt deeply rejected . . . but he had an energetic stubbornness which is at the bottom of all his characters. Some other guy would just give it all up. But he continued to write.

When I think of it objectively, I'm awed by it. Rejection at the age of fifty and dragging his family down with him. In his mind, he had become like one of his characters, a bum, a literary bum. In the middle of it all, he suffered horrendous financial difficulties. But through it all, he would climb up there and just plug away.[54]

Kennedy even compares his own determination with Bailey's, the protagonist of *The Ink Truck:* Bailey's "kind of insane perseverance was the heart of what I felt I was going through in the sixties. It was a dismal, defeated period for Bailey, and so it was for me."[55] Kennedy's principal protagonists—Bailey, Jack Diamond, Daniel Quinn, and Billy and Francis Phelan—reflect a similar perseverance and determination to "survive" and become "warriors" who strive to become "something valuable in life" and who "sustain a serious attitude toward survival. It's always a war—you're at war with somebody or, as in Francis' case, a war of the spirit."[56] Kennedy's dedication to writing probably can be explained by Saul Bellow's remark about *character:* "Talent goes a certain distance. The rest of the writer's life has to be carried by character."[57]

Bellow never explained precisely what he meant by *character*, and Kennedy interpreted it as the "pursuit of art—refusal to yield to failure, refusal to accept any kind of rejection and let that define your life."[58] Kennedy even advises would-be writers regarding dedication and perseverance:

Don't trust your mentor, your teacher, your mother or any critic who either praises or damns you. Trust yourself, even when you are most certain that you have no luck, no talent, no imagination, no money, and no literary future. Let your subconscious make all the heavy decisions about the future. If you go back to the writing table after abysmal, hellish failure in the eyes of everyone around you, you, friend, are a baptized, circumcised, confirmed and bar mitzvah'd writer. Toast yourself. It's a glorious moment of self-recognition. Have another. You'll need it.[59]

Chapter Two

"A Town with a Smudged Soul": *O Albany!*

William Kennedy's *O Albany! Improbable City of Political Wizards, Fearless Ethnics, Spectacular Aristocrats, Splendid Nobodies, and Underrated Scoundrels*[1] evolved from a series of articles Kennedy wrote for the *Albany Times Union*. "I always wanted to reprint those essays," says Kennedy, "because I felt they had permanent value to a lot of people for Albany."[2] Susanne Dumbleton and Anne Older had started The Washington Park Press in Albany and were interested in publishing the articles, so Kennedy signed a contract for "the sumptuous amount of $500" (Letter, 29 April 1988). After Kennedy reread the articles, however, he realized that "twenty years had elapsed and a lot of things had changed including my prose style, and I couldn't abide most of them, and obviously I had to do a lot more reporting."[3] Kennedy then wrote *O Albany!* in ten or eleven months, but, he emphasizes, "outside of the sections on Union Station, 'The Democrats Convene,' and 'Capitol Hill: A Visit with the Pruyn Family,' all writing was done from scratch, and those old newspaper articles became merely raw material for the new chapters" (Letter, 29 April 1988). Although *O Albany!* was originally intended as a "paperback for local consumption," Kennedy says, "as I wrote the book it became obvious that there was more here than local color. There were indeed national patterns and microcosms to be tracked and the melting pot of American history, plus specialty items such as the Kenmore, and Diamond, that obviously had wide appeal. As the book was being finished, I convinced Sue and Anne that we should try to have Viking publish it and so the book became a joint venture between Washington Park Press and Viking" (Letter, 29 April 1988).

In *O Albany!*'s opening essay, Kennedy quotes Stanford White, who called Albany the "most miserable" of all the "wretched second-class, one-horse towns," and John Gunter, who called Albany a "kind of political *cloaca maxima*, beside which Kansas City seemed almost pure" (*OA*, 3). In an apologia for Albany, however, Kennedy declares that *O Albany!* is an "attempt to strike a balance as to Albany's legend. Even iniquity has its charms: consider what Milton did with Satan. But I am fond of things beyond the city's iniquity. I love its times of grace and greatness, its political secrets, and its historical presence in every facet of the nation's life . . . It is centered squarely in the American continuum, a magical place where the past becomes visible if one is willing to track the multiple incarnations of the city's soul" (*OA*, 4, 7). If the *O Albany!* essays locate Albany in the human and American continuum as Kennedy traces the city's soul, then so, too, do his novels. The *O Albany!* essays are significant, therefore, because they "serve as a kind of Baedeker to the world of Kennedy's novels,"[4] and because they use literary techniques and themes that are evident in his novels.

As a Baedeker to Kennedy's Fiction

Albany's historical context is one guide to Kennedy's fiction, and in "Albany as a State of Mind," Kennedy writes, "I confront even a single street corner and there emerges an archetypal as well as an historical context in which to view the mutations of its trees, its telephone poles" (*OA*, 7). In this sense, too, the *O Albany!* essays establish historical contexts that form the backdrops in front of which his fictional characters live and act. In reviewing *O Albany!*, James W. Oberly writes that the book is composed "in part" of the "nonfictional stories" that Kennedy creates in his novels.[5] Although these essays need not be read in conjunction with the novels, the essays do add an historical dimension to the Albany of his fiction and provide a context for his fictional characters. For example, *Legs* is Kennedy's reinvention of Jack Diamond, but in *O Albany!*, "Prohibition: It Can't Happen Here" and "The Death of Legs Diamond" augment the fictional portrait with an historical dimension. Similarly, the fictional portraits of the McCalls and their political machinations in *Billy Phelan's Greatest Game* gain credibility from the *O Albany!* essays, "The Democrats Convene, or, One Man's Family" and "They Bury the Boss: Dan Ex-Machina." On the other hand, *Quinn's Book* is a retrospective Baedeker that not only enriches Kennedy's other novels and a great many *O Albany!* essays, but also benefits from knowledge of the earlier novels and essays. Furthermore, as in the novels, historical events and people's lives interconnect the *O Albany!* essays. For example, while Legs Diamond and Dan O'Connell are focal points in their respective essays, each may be mentioned briefly in other essays. Moreover, even these brief references augment the historical portraits in *O Albany!* and the fictional portraits in the novels.

As a part of American history, Prohibition figures prominently in Albany's past. According to Kennedy, Prohibition in Albany "was a contradiction in terms" because very little was prohibited in this city, a "place where you could restore your spirit or smudge your soul" (*OA*, 189), a comment equally applicable to other American cities of the era. Although drinking in Albany had been a favorite pastime as far back as 1653, Kennedy wryly notes that "drinking exploded ridiculously in the 1920s when people were told they couldn't drink . . . People who didn't drink at all, drank a little bit" (*OA*, 190). Indeed, Albany experienced a burgeoning of speakeasies during Prohibition because, to quote Kennedy, "All you needed to create a speakeasy was two bottles and a room, and Albany had hundreds" (*OA*, 193), including the 21 Club; King Brady's in Kennedy's North Albany, a particularly wet neighborhood; the Parody Club, one of Jack Diamond's haunts; and the Blue Heaven, a former saloon opened and operated by Kennedy's great-grandfather, Big Jim Carroll. As long as there was no public drunkenness or violence, the Albany speakeasies thrived, serving beer and whiskey transported by trucks, one of which had a flat tire that was replaced by a police repair crew in an effort that Kennedy describes as "civic cooperation" (*OA*, 192).

During Prohibition, political corruption and mob-world links prevailed in both Albany and other major cities. "The gangster as the assuager of thirst," writes Kennedy, "was an important man to American society in the 1920s, and Albany knew him well . . . Dutch Schultz, Waxey Gordon, Vincent Coll, Fats McCarthy, Lucky Luciano, and numerous lesser-known hoodlums—they all played roles on our local stage" (*OA*, 190–91). What was singular about Albany during Prohibition, however, was Dan O'Connell's power that could and did keep the gangsters out of Albany, thus sparing the city the gangster world's most unsavory aspect, its gang wars. O'Connell had personal reasons for his civic zeal—he selected his own booze kingpins and had his own truck garage that dispensed illegal whiskey and beer. After Prohibition, O'Connell opened Hedrick's Brewery, which prospered since he undersold his competitors, and proprietors "stacked it up in the cellar rather than offend Dan, and by way of reciprocation, Dan's authorities looked the other way when these proprietors extended their drinking hours beyond legal limits" (*OA*, 198).

Legs Diamond, the flamboyant gangster of the Roaring Twenties, figures prominently in America's and Albany's annals, and Kennedy complements the fictional portrait of Diamond in *Legs* with a factual account in "The Death of Legs Diamond." For example, Diamond often partied at the Kenmore Hotel's Rain-Bo Room where he had his own table and where "nobody sat there but him and about six bodyguards and his girl, Kiki Roberts. Nobody gave him any trouble. And he paid. And did he get service" (*OA*,

185). Diamond's presence in Albany became especially evident in 1931 while he was recovering in Albany Hospital after another assassination attempt and awaiting trial for kidnapping Grover Parks. Diamond's lawyer was Daniel H. Prior, a former Albany judge and lawyer who would become part of the basis for Marcus Gorman's characterization in *Legs*. Diamond also allegedly had dealings with John and Francis Oley, two of Albany's most famous criminal hall-of-famers from the old Cabbagetown neighborhood. Diamond's most permanent link with Albany occurred when he was murdered on 18 December 1931 at 67 Dove Street, a house which Kennedy purchased. In a dramatic and fictional touch, Kennedy's essay about Diamond's death swells the myth by emphasizing that Diamond's murderers were "never identified, though they were heard, probably seen, their car definitely seen, the pistols they used found in the neighborhood" (*OA*, 202), all of which highlights the speculations about Diamond's possible murderers: Dutch Schultz, Lucky Luciano, Bo Weinberg, Fats McCarthy, Vincent Coll. According to Kennedy, however, William J. Fitzpatrick, an Albany policeman who eventually became Chief of Police, killed Diamond, probably on Dan O'Connell's orders. Adding another historical dimension to Diamond's legend without altering his fictional portrait in *Legs*, Kennedy concludes his Diamond essay on a mysterious note: "All of this hardly closes the case on who shot Jack [Diamond], but what it does do is give equal time to the police. For it wasn't backroom gossip among reporters, politicians, and old-time hoodlums that brought the skeleton out of the closet. It was Dan the man. 'Fitzpatrick finished Legs,' is what he said" (*OA*, 210).

Another historical fact is Albany's Nighttown, the backdrop for *Ironweed* and particularly for *Billy Phelan's Greatest Game*. Kennedy captures Nighttown's ambiance, gaudy glitter and seamier nuances in the opening of "Sports and Swells":

If you were a Damon Runyon sort of sport, up until the 1940s you'd have hung out in the center of Nighttown, which was Broadway—a block long, between Steuben and Columbia streets—directly across from Union Station. The block was home to some famous places, including the Famous Lunch, the American Tavern (which had been Schlitz's Hotel), Brockley's grill, the Cadillac Hotel, Swift Mead's Saloon, Rinaldi's fruit store for when you needed a banana, and Joe Preiss's pawnshop for when you went broke. The night world sprawled outward from Union Station's block—down Broadway and up State Street and up Hudson Avenue, up Columbia to North Pearl, up Broadway to Little Harlem, down Green Street into an assortment of back alleys and shadowy streets where you could make your fortune for the week, or lose your virginity or your dignity with Big Betty, or if she wasn't how you wanted to lose whatever it was you needed to lose, you could try Madge Burn's house, or Little Read's, or Davenport's, which was the expensive place, five dollars a shot. So they say. (*OA*, 179–80)

This description complements the descriptions of Broadway in *Billy Phelan's Greatest Game*, especially in the opening pages of Chapter 8.

Moreover, "Sports and Swells" touches upon another aspect of Albany's night life, the fabled Rain-Bo Room in the Kenmore Hotel. The Rain-Bo Room opened in 1922 and enjoyed its heyday between 1929 and 1939. Somewhat similar to Harlem's Cotton Club in its style of entertainment and in its ultimate fate, the Rain-Bo Room featured headline performers: Duke Ellington, Cab Calloway, Benny Goodman, Guy Lombardo, Tommy Dorsey with vocalist Frank Sinatra, Red Nichols and the Five Pennies, Jack and Charlie Teagarden, Bix Beiderbecke, and Sophie Tucker. In entertainment firsts, entrepreneur and owner Bob Murphy inaugurated national broadcasts of the Rain-Bo Room's big bands, instituted the first minimum check charge policy in the United States, advertised " 'never a cover charge' and business boomed anew" (*OA*, 186).

As another historical presence in Albany's history, Daniel P. O'Connell and his Irish–Democratic political machine were the subject of "The Democrats Convene," "They Bury the Boss: Dan Ex-Machina," and "Erastus: The Million Dollar Smile" about Mayor Erastus Corning, who served forty-one years in office. Indeed, the *Booklist* reviewer notes that Albany's story is primarily one of "machine politics, and Kennedy rightly devotes much of his book to the two men who made the city's democratic machine run for six decades: Dan O'Connell and Erastus Corning."[6] Kennedy notes that the O'Connell and Corning material has been the "most fascinating of all pieces" to write.[7]

Dan O'Connell was elected as an Albany assessor by 145 votes in 1919, and thus began the rise of O'Connell's political machine operated by Dan and his brothers: Patrick "Packy" O'Connell, First Ward Democratic leader; John "Solly" O'Connell, overseer of Albany's Nighttown; and Edward O'Connell, a lawyer who was "coequal with Dan in running the Albany Democratic Party" (*OA*, 91). So powerful, organized, and influential was the O'Connell machine that it not only carried Albany's elections, but it also influenced both the New York gubernatorial elections and the nation's presidential primaries. Governor Mario Cuomo even attested to Dan O'Connell's "wizardry with elections" in an anecdote in which O'Connell and another man were marooned on an island with only one coconut between them. In a vote to see who would eat the coconut, "Dan won, 110 to 1" (*OA*, 286)—no doubt another reason for Kennedy's referring to Dan O'Connell as "Dan Ex-Machina." Despite its good points—keeping gangsters out of Albany, providing the "dole when there was no job, the loan when there was no dole, the security of the neighborhood, the new streetlight, the new sidewalk" (*OA*, 45) —the O'Connell machine was rife with corruption although several investigations resulted in very few convictions.

Repeated allegations of vote buying and ballot stuffing reveal the corruption: "In Albany, it was rumored, even the dead voted, early and often" (*OA*, 293). In another instance, gubernatorial candidate Thomas E. Dewey accused the O'Connell machine of voting fraud: "They have registered 82,000 people in Albany, and that's 3,000 more than the *City Directory* could find" (*OA*, 286). Moreover, since Solly O'Connell ruled Albany's Nighttown, taxes were raised or lowered and laws bent slightly depending on whether merchants or businessmen supported or opposed the O'Connells' power. As a case in point, the Albany Senators' baseball management housed the opposing teams in Bob Murphy's Kenmore Hotel until Murphy "backed the wrong political candidate in the early 1930s, fell from favor with the O'Connells, and found out that the Senators no longer saw fit to use his premises. You're out, Murphy" (*OA*, 185).

Another historical fact that finds its way into Kennedy's fiction was the kidnapping of Dan O'Connell's nephew, John, Solly's son, on 7 July 1933 in front of the home at 14 Putnam Street. John Jr., like his characterization Charles McCall in *Billy Phelan's Greatest Game*, was held in New Jersey. Although John Jr.'s kidnappers demanded $250,000 ransom, they eventually settled for $40,000, and Manny Strewel was the alleged disinterested go-between (in *Billy Phelan*, the go-between is Morrie Berman). The eight kidnappers were apprehended and sentenced to long prison terms. Manny Strewel's fifty-eight year sentence was later reduced to twenty-two years; Thomas Dugan, John McClone, Charles Harrigan, George Garguillo, Percy Geary, and John Oley received seventy-eight year sentences; Francis Oley hanged himself in his cell shortly after his arrest. Kennedy reports that any Albany policeman who helped in the investigation, "found himself a likely candidate for promotion in later years on the force, for Dan had a long and grateful memory" (*OA*, 48).

Other historical contexts that weave their way into Kennedy's fiction are the cholera epidemics, the Delavan Hotel fire, the 1913 flood that inundated Broadway, the New York Central railroad shops and yards, the iron foundries, the Irish immigration, and the 1901 United Traction strike against trolleys in five cities: "Albany was put under martial law, troops camped at Beverwyck Park, and a squad of soldiers rode on every streetcar. E. LeRoy

Smith and William M. Walsh were killed when troops opened fire on a violent mob attacking a car at Columbia Street and Broadway. Smith was standing in the doorway of a store, watching the riot, when he was shot" (*OA*, 63). *O Albany!* offers other pieces of Albany's history that, while just as entertaining and informative, are too numerous to cover in this study. With its combination of history and personal memoirs about Albany's great and not-so-great moments, *O Albany!* has become, as Kennedy says, "a labor of love" and "an amalgam of everything I had done as a journalist over many years" and which "just seemed to fall into place when I began to pay close attention to the structure of the book."[8] Although Peter Quinn claims that *O Albany!* "stands on its own" and need not be read "in connection" with Kennedy's other novels,[9] Christopher Lehmann-Haupt writes, "Even more amazing than the detail and the enthusiasm is the raw material of Mr. Kennedy's fiction present on every page. Even if one doesn't give a damn for Albany, it is always interesting to watch the author's imagination at play in the city and its history, for one is witnessing the first step in the novelist's creative process."[10] Most of the *O Albany!* essays were written, however, after Kennedy had published his first three novels and had even finished writing *Ironweed*. While Lehmann-Haupt's contention that *O Albany!* reflects the first steps in Kennedy's creative process may be misinformed, the *O Albany!* essays, though journalistic, contain his fictional techniques, especially in their dramatic scenes, use of dialogue, status detail, complex and inventive points of view, dramatic opening sentences, structures, and understatements.[11]

Kennedy often uses dramatic scenes in *O Albany!*, and they are particularly evident in "The Gut: Our Boulevard of Bluest Dreams" in which Olivia Rorie talks about her neighborhood, as well as in "The Death of Legs Diamond" featuring the description of Diamond's death and the murder of Detective William J. Fitzpatrick by John W. McElveney, a fellow Albany detective. Most of the essays use dialogue, but the most memorable example occurs in "Italians" in which Andy Viglucci remembers his grandmother who always dressed in black—"in mourning for relatives, for kids who didn't make it over from Italy, for everybody she knew"—and who always said to him, "Howsa you? Andrew eat. No makea skinny, makea fat. Shut up, eat" (*OA*, 241). Status details appear in Dan O'Connell's "three-inch-brim fedora" that betokened his political power, and in "Capitol Hill: A Visit with the Pruyn Family" in which Hubertie Pruyn describes her family's typical dinnerware and fare.

As do his novels, Kennedy's *O Albany!* essays reveal complex and inventive points of view. For example, "The West End: Money on the Hoof, Money on Wheels" opens with: "If it were morning again on a summer day in one of the last years of the last century, a young boy might get out of bed in his home at Number 8 Watervliet Avenue and look out the window to watch the cattle go by in the street" (*OA*, 130). After generalizing about the boy's father who lost his job with the New York Central Railroad during the 1890 strike and about how the boy may play ball behind the railroad YMCA or watch the ice melt that was harvested in the winter, Kennedy identifies the boy as Leo Brennan, who is now "seventy-one, longtime clerk of Albany's Traffic Court and resident of the West End all his life" (*OA*, 131). After excursions into historical perspectives about the West End, its people, businesses, and changes, Kennedy returns to Leo Brennan, then introduces Brennan's friends, John Parsons and Jim Meany, who also become pivotal points for describing other West End happenings. Brennan, Parsons, and Meany thus emerge as factual characters about whom real events swirl. Their reminiscences and reactions provide, moreover, personal insights into Albany's history. Similar techniques enliven other *O Albany!* essays: "Legacy from a Lady" and "North Albany: Crucible for a Childhood" in which Kennedy relates his own experiences; "The Bowery: Cabbages, Plucks, and Bloodsuckers" in which John Pauly, John R. Hauf, and Dan Corr take center stage; and "Downtown: Where Things Happened First" in which Tim Lyden, who at seventy-four had lived most of his life in Albany's downtown section, becomes the focus.

The *O Albany!* essays open with dramatic beginning sentences, a common journalistic device. In *Letter to a Would-Be Journalist*, a module for a journalism course, Kennedy advises the student about dramatic opening sentences: "THE LEAD: The point of the lead is to drag you into a story, grab you by the eyeballs and force you to keep reading. It should shock, amuse, inform, enlighten, intrigue . . . for instance . . . at a St. Patrick's day party: 'There were shamrocks on every table. They were potted too.' "[12] In commenting about a journalistic series entitled "The Slums of Albany," Kennedy emphasizes that " 'The Slums of Albany are a horror' was the opening line, and things went from there down to rat level" (*OA*, 252). Moreover, in *O Albany!*, "The Death of Legs Diamond" begins with: "Jack (Legs) Diamond, the most visible, most maligned, and most famous criminal in the East throughout the latter years of Prohibition, was Albany's preeminent underworld celebrity" (*OA*, 199). Equally dramatic is the opening of "The Democrats Convene, or, One Man's Family": "Ah yes, Dan O'Connell. He was Jesus Christ in baggy pants and a brown three-inch-brim fedora that some people like John Lindsay thought was a cowboy hat. But it was a political hat, and the head of the savior of all Albany Democrats was under it" (*OA*, 43). Besides answering the journalistic who-what-where-when questions, the de-

tails also suggest O'Connell's imposing presence and political power, qualities reinforced by the opening paragraph's last three sentences: "When it appeared in public it told the faithful, 'It's all right, boys and girls, nothing's
changed. I've still got the same hat. And the city and county, too" (*OA*, 43).
In "The Romance of the Oriflamme," Kennedy introduces Albany's ties with
the magic of railroads and trains with: "Union Station was magical because it
was more than itself, which is how it is with any magical man, woman, or
building" (*OA*, 17).

Another literary technique in *O Albany!* is its circular structures. *O
Albany!* begins with Kennedy's personal recollections in "Albany as a State of
Mind" and ends with his reminiscences about his parents, their courtship,
and eventual marriage in "Albany as a Pair of Suspenders and a Movie."
Kennedy writes, "I take it Mary McDonald found a way to let Bill Kennedy
know she was at leisure. And they did step out. I am here to tell about that"
(*OA*, 384). The individual essays also build circular structures. "The Democrats Convene," for instance, begins with Dan O'Connell's arrival in his
"baggy pants" and famous fedora and ends with his departure from Polish
Hall. "Arbor Hill: Yesterday's Arcadia" opens with "Arbor Hill is the most
mercurial of Albany's neighborhoods" and closes with "Then the world
would change again; Arbor Hill would grow old and become expendable in a
new way" (*OA*, 96, 105).

One entertaining device that Kennedy uses in *O Albany!* originates either
in literature's understatement or journalism's "caboose," identified by journalist James J. Kilpatrick as a sentence that "packs its unexpected wallop at
the end."[13] Whether understatement or "caboose," the result is usually de-
lightfully humorous. In "Prohibition: It Can't Happen Here," for example,
Kennedy writes that Robert A. Corradini, then a research secretary for the
World League Against Alcoholism, noted not only a decline in drinking, but
also a decline in profanity "since people tended not to curse and swear outside
of saloons" (*OA*, 193). Kennedy records another Prohibition irony in writing
about Jack McEneny, an Albany commissioner who told of a miracle involving several barrels of whiskey confiscated and held in Central Avenue's Fifth
Precinct: "Overnight . . . inside the police station every barrel's contents had
turned to water" (*OA*, 195). Regarding Albany's voting scandals, Kennedy
relates another ironically humorous incident in the 1940s when one of
Dewey's investigators found a house where supposedly seventy-eight voters
lived but which had only twenty-two cots, an inconsistency explained by the
proprietor who claimed that "the voters slept in eight-hour shifts." Kennedy
wryly adds, "That still left twelve who had to sleep standing up" (*OA*, 308).
Kennedy does not place himself above the humor, either. In relating the

voguish places to eat in Albany's Pine Hills section, Kennedy says that he was not aware that the Washington Tavern had become an Irish bar until proprietor Mike Byron "betrayed his ethnicity" by serving Kennedy a "free plate of corned beef and cabbage," and says Kennedy, "I betrayed my own by eating it" (*OA*, 127).

Kennedy's wit surfaces in various ways. In relating the details about Albany's last public execution in which Jesse Strang was hanged for murdering his lover's husband, Kennedy writes, "Sheriff Conrad A. Ten Eyck cut the rope drop, and then Jesse Strang, he swang" (*OA*, 87). In describing Treasury agents, Kennedy writes, "T-men . . . in those days were as alphabetically important as G-men" (*OA*, 249). In describing how on cold, icy days the downhill trolley jumped its tracks and crashed into either the Grace Methodist Church or the home of the Sixth Ward's Democratic leader, Kennedy proves "that neither God nor the Democratic party had any control over the traction interests" (*OA*, 105). In writing about the Young Men's Italian Association's efforts to campaign "against an image the members felt degraded all Italians, the organ grinder as beggar," Kennedy says that the legislation failed to pass and the "organ grinder continued to pump away at his monkey business until the organ finally broke down, or maybe the radio drowned him out" (*OA*, 237–38).

Until the Organ Broke Down: Themes

To consider this ending of "Italians" in *O Albany!*—"to pump away at his monkey business until the organ finally broke down, or maybe the radio drowned him out"—is to become aware that *O Albany!* is about endings, the end of an era or the end of a way of life. In "The West End: Money on the Hoof, Money on Wheels," for example, Jim Meany reflects on the decline of the great railroad shops and their eventual closings and says, "It's a way of life that's passed on . . . That's all, it's passed on" (*OA*, 141). "Sports and Swells" focuses on Nighttown's famous restaurants that included the Delavan House, the Rain-Bo Room, and Keeler's, and the essay ends with: "On November 17, 1969, a sign appeared on Keeler's door. CLOSED, it said. Sports and swells everywhere cried in their beer" (*OA*, 188). In "The Last Word," the essay about Mayor Erastus Corning's death, Kennedy concludes with: "There the O'Connell–Corning Machine goes off the air, and the rest is memory and hearsay" (*OA*, 371).[14] These references document one theme in *O Albany!*—the end of an era and the end of a way of life.

Nor are endings and closings relegated always to the essays' closing paragraphs. In "Jews," for instance, Kennedy writes, "After the war the South End

Jewish neighborhood began its final decline," and concerning the decline of
Albany's German enclave because of the antipathy of World Wars I and II,
Kennedy writes that the "more significant loss was the disappearance of the
German newspapers that had chronicled the life of the Germans in the city
from the beginning of the immigration" (*OA,* 228, 250). Indeed, the passing
of people, institutions, and ways of life is nowhere better depicted than in
Kennedy's comment about the closing of the Rain-Bo Room:

All gone: Berigan, Murphy, Prior; Broadway and the gamblers also gone; both
Keelers gone. And at the end of the Rain-Bo there wasn't even a pot. Bob Murphy
remembered that the federal government slapped a 20 percent excise tax on entertainment after World War II. The Big Band Era was fading; rising union scales sent
music costs soaring. "People resented the tax," Murphy said. "Then the money got
short and television came in." Nobody came to the Kenmore, and in 1947 Albany's
greatest nightclub closed its gate on history. (*OA,* 187)

Closings and endings are, however, only part of the theme in *O Albany!*.
    In reviewing *O Albany!*, Thomas Fleming points out that the book "recalls
how many reincarnations Albany and the rest of America has undergone in
the 370 years since a handful of Dutchmen sailed up the Hudson to open a
fur trading post . . . So many flourishings, fadings, deaths and rebirths.
Albany has been counted out a dozen times—with the disappearance of the
fur trade, the waning of the Erie Canal, the collapse of the railroads, the evis-
ceration of its downtown section. Each time it has returned to improbable
life."[15] William Kennedy, of course, records these rebirths and resurrections
in this "improbable city." As an instance, in "The Romance of the
Oriflamme," an essay about Albany's once grand Union Station, Kennedy
writes that in "1983, Union Station is the on-again, off-again centerpiece of a
$100 million hotel and thirty-story office building project"—and then con-
cludes the essay with a hint of the station's magic: "But the romance of the
oriflamme is dead. So surely and thoroughly gone, was it a trick then? Oh no"
(*OA,* 20, 21). Similarly, "The Gut: Our Boulevard of Bluest Dreams" ends
with the efforts to restore an Albany neighborhood to its grand eloquence:
"Millions were being spent to create these streets as the Pastures, the city's
newest and oldest and most ironic neighborhood," a fate paralleling that of
Arbor Hill which the "urban Fates" are restoring to the "sunny and tree-lined
garden that existed when the world was young and beautiful" (*OA,* 175,
266). There is also the South Mall that denigrators labeled "City Beautiful's
last erection" or "Rockefeller's last erection" since Governor Nelson
Rockefeller ramrodded its concept and construction. Despite its construction

frauds and overruns and its "destruction of 1,150 structures, most of them private dwellings, the displacement of 3,600 households," Kennedy believes the South Mall is largely responsible for the "Albany turnaround," a claim he supports with statistics about how many people jam the mall for its cultural and tourist attractions (*OA*, 306, 307, 321).

O Albany!'s themes of change and resurrection loosely relate to the themes of restoration and regeneration evident in Kennedy's novels. Moreover, Kennedy's *O Albany!* essays, like his novels, hint of the magical. For instance, "Albany as a State of Mind" concludes with Kennedy's promise to trace Albany's past as it "turns so magically . . . from then into now." In "The Democrats Convene," as Dan O'Connell leaves the Polish Hall a sense of magic pervades the scene: "Then the sun turned emerald green and settled itself heavily behind the rooftops of Gander Bay. Ghosts of geese and ganders waddled in their ease. There was and there would be no storm on this blessedly peaceful night" (*OA*, 53).

As in this description of the "blessedly peaceful night," Kennedy often testifies, either directly or indirectly, to his sense of some kind of magic at work in the world. *O Albany!*'s "Part I" is entitled "Magical Places," and in some essays Albany becomes a "magical place" where the past turns "so magically" from then into now. In "The Romance of the Oriflamme," Union Station "was magical from the beginning," especially on its debut day, "everything that day was magical." In *O Albany!* and the novels, the *magic* is neither ominous nor supernatural, but rather it suggests the hopeful potential for restoration, recycling, or regeneration that, despite the inevitability of change, exists in modern life. Thus Albany has the potential for restoring and recycling its neighborhoods and downtown area. Or, to quote Kennedy, "Renewal . . . it's a constant regeneration of the city by various ethnic groups and political powers—Dan O'Connell passing, Erastus Corning passing on, and Arbor Hill going through its escalations."[16]

Kennedy writes that Albany is "centered squarely in the American and human continuum," and its place in the continuum results from both its history and its recyclings and restorations, all of which are typified in a passage from "Downtown: Where Things Happened First":

The permanent population hit its lowest point in the 1960s for Downtown had become a wasteland . . . Downtown's moribund commerce in a few more years would finally die entirely and go to heaven in the suburban Colonie Center—one of the ten more successful shopping malls in the U.S. The Ten Eyck Hotel would die and on the dust of its bones a few years later the Albany Hilton would be rising. The DeWitt Clinton Hotel would die as a hotel and become an apartment house, chockablock with senior citizens . . . Columbia Street . . . would, by the late 1970s, have its houses restored to Victorian respectability and families would be moving back to Downtown streets, alive again with trees and quickened traffic. Largely because of the South Mall, every salvageable town house or row house would become a target for rehabilitation. City living, in the age of the shortage and inflated price of gasoline, would once again be chic. (*OA,* 61).

This summarizes the histories of virtually all American cities—Boston, Baltimore, Atlanta, Kansas City, San Francisco. At the same time, the restoration of Albany's Union Station and its vicinity mirrors the restoration of St. Louis' Union Station and Little Rock's Union Station. Although Kennedy writes in *O Albany!* that the Kenmore Hotel may or may not have a future,[17] other grand hotels have been restored to their former grace and elegance, most notably the Hotel Peabody in Memphis, Tennessee; the Omni Hotel in St. Louis; the Capitol Hotel in Little Rock, Arkansas; and so goes the list. In *O Albany!,* Kennedy not only depicts Albany's uniqueness, but he also transcends the city limits to suggest its universality in the human and American continuums. Indeed, Albany may have its cloacal moments, but it also has its moments of magic, greatness, and grace. Albany is, as Kennedy reports, "a hot town, a crazy town, a town with a smudged soul, but a town with a soul to besmudge" (*OA,* 198).

Chapter Three
"Out of the Late 1960s": *The Ink Truck*

Generally, reviewers and critics fault William Kennedy's *The Ink Truck* for its stylistic inadequacies. E. A. Dooley, for example, believes that the novel's action is "too jumpy" and concludes that Kennedy is a "skilled weaver of words" but should concentrate on "straight picturesque writing rather than on mystifying fantasy."[1] Stanley Reynolds denigratingly writes that the "novel has the look of something typed in dull moments around the newspaper office" and that "one feels that Mr. Kennedy was unfortunate to have had the free time to finish his 'comic masterpiece.' "[2] In contrast, Dorothy Curley remarks that Kennedy's "aims and characters are sympathetic" and recommends *The Ink Truck* as an "intriguing first novel for large collections."[3] Shane Stevens praises *The Ink Truck* as imaginative, "inventive, circular and multi-layered" with characters "as real as they are symbolic, the scenes as much reality as fantasy . . . Kennedy has been able to confine his wickedly surrealist imagination within a well-told tale. The result is a Dantean journey through the hells of existence."[4]

When it was reissued after *Ironweed's* success, later reviewers noted that *The Ink Truck* presaged Kennedy's later and greater novels. While remarking that Kennedy was not "skillful enough" at the time "to create a sympathetic protagonist," Anne Tyler claims that *The Ink Truck* is a "finger exercise for the Albany cycle."[5] According to Loxley F. Nichols, *The Ink Truck* contains many elements that "later became his trademark," a "predominantly Irish (American) world of unsuspected heroes, lost causes, and errant pookas."[6] Joel Conarroe says that it contains "numerous thematic links with the later books" and reveals "an energetic but as yet undisciplined artist working his way somewhat clumsily to the flexible style that would become his trademark."[7]

The Ink Truck does contain minor stylistic flaws but critics and reviewers did not see the novel as a fictional rendering of the age in which it was written. Kennedy says, "*The Ink Truck* is a book that grows out of the late 1960s and it absorbs a lot of the radical atmosphere of the time: the hippie movement, the drug movement, the sexual revolution, the crazy politics, all the death and assassination . . . My book doesn't reflect these things directly but they helped to make the book what it is."[8] To analyze *The Ink Truck,* therefore, as part of the literature of the 1960s is to gain a clearer insight into its plot, characters, setting, and themes.

Literature and the 1960s: Some Overviews

In a retrospective glance at the fiction of the 1960s, Peter S. Prescott generalizes about the characteristics of the best American fiction of this decade. Among these characteristics, three apply to *The Ink Truck:* there is logic in lunacy; the individual feels impotent when confronting society; and although the writers believe that the world is past saving, "men may save themselves; not by the preachments and methodologies we have developed only to see them betray us, but by returning to the humanity in each of us."[9] In generalizing about the 1960s and American fiction, James E. Miller lists four characteristics: "the nightmare world, alienation and nausea, the quest for identity, the comic doomsday vision"—and then adds a fifth one: "a thin, frail line of hope," or the "kind of affirmation found in such novels as Heller's *Catch-22* and Kesey's *One Flew Over the Cuckoo's Nest*—the defiant assertion of one's humanity in the face of overwhelming forces that dehumanize and destroy."[10] Complementing these overviews are Will Herberg's insights into Mass Society, a society of "vast anonymous masses in which the individual is stripped bare of whatever peculiarities of background, tradition, and social position . . . and converted into a homogenized, featureless unit in a vast impersonal machine" that erodes person-to-person relationships and creates a "non-involved sociability."[11] Finally, the 1960s hero is alienated and isolated in an absurd world marked by topsy-turvy values and beliefs, inconsistencies, and often surrealistic, nightmarish fantasies, and in such a world the hero must assert his individual dignity and significance and find purpose and meaning in his life, or, to mimic one protest cry of the sixties, "I am a human being! Do not fold, spindle, or mutilate!"

In plot, character, and theme, Ken Kesey's *One Flew Over the Cuckoo's Nest* and Joseph Heller's *Catch-22* resemble Kennedy's *The Ink Truck*—Stanley Reynolds even claims that *The Ink Truck* is in the "fashionable mode of *Catch-22* or Vonnegut."[12] Moreover, *Cuckoo's Nest* and *Catch-22* typify the fiction of the 1960s in their depictions of Mass Society; absurd, surrealistic worlds; and isolated, alienated heroes defiantly battling overwhelming, dehumanizing forces. In *Catch-22,* the vast military system represents Mass Society; in *Cuckoo's Nest,* the Combine, the hospital ward, and the Big Nurse represent Mass Society. Similarly, a refusal to become involved appears in

Catch-22 in Major Major's refusal to ground combat-fatigued flyers, and especially in the men who pop out of the bushes and wait to see if Yossarian will be punished for refusing to fly more missions; in *Cuckoo's Nest* the patients spy on each other and refuse to help each other during the Big Nurse's emasculating group therapy sessions. Both novels also depict absurd worlds as reflected in the Big Nurse's ward policies and in the catch-22 dilemma.

As an isolated, alienated character, Yossarian, the protagonist of *Catch-22,* wants to survive the war and has tried various alternatives that range wackily from completing the required number of missions and malingering in the hospital to moving the bomb line and finally deserting. Because of his eccentricities and constant cry, "They're trying to kill me," other characters either ignore him or call him *crazy* or *madman.* Randle Patrick McMurphy, the protagonist of *Cuckoo's Nest,* feigns insanity so that he can substitute the easy life on the ward for the hard manual labor on a prison work farm. In their absurd worlds, neither Yossarian nor McMurphy is mad but rather trapped by an establishment whose leaders are insane and inhumane. One character in *Catch-22* says that Yossarian is probably the only sane one in the squadron, and McMurphy tells the patients that they may be eccentric but they are not "nuts." Finally, because McMurphy and Yossarian adamantly oppose the establishment, both are offered compromises that damn either way—"damned if you do and damned if you don't," says a character in *Cuckoo's Nest*—and in refusing compromise, they typify Miller's "thin, frail line of hope."

The 1960s and *The Ink Truck*

One characteristic of the 1960s literature in *The Ink Truck* is the absurd world. Kennedy says, "The silliness of the strike and the absence of achievement as a result of the strike, the threats of violence—they shaped the making of that book."[13] For example, the strikers' demands and the company's counterdemands blur as the strike continues. The Guild begins asking for $292 a week, the newspaper refuses, and so negotiations wackily range from a cut back on paid holidays and charging lunches at the company coffee shop to splitting tuxedo rental fees with the newspaper covering formal functions: "reporters are notorious gravy spillers and must pay for their own dress shirt and jacket."[14] As the bickerings drag on, salary demands are about forty percent below prestrike demands. Other examples of the absurd include Miss Blue's toro-machine, the two-car motocade, and Bailey's willful shelving of library books with their backs to the wall. In addition, *Catch-22* absurdities echo in some of the situations and dialogue. After Bailey refuses to apologize to Stanley and returns to the parking lot, the attendant orders Bailey to move his car. But someone has stolen its engine which prompts the attendant to claim, "We're not responsible for articles left in the car that get lost or stolen" (*IT,* 125). The craziest example of absurd dialogue occurs when Bailey begins his solitary picketing and Jarvis tells him that the Guild is no longer picketing:

> "That lets me out. I'm not in the Guild."
> "Then why the heck are you picketing?"
> "Because I'm on strike."
> "You can't picket if you're not in the Guild."
> "Are you in the Guild, Jarvis?"
> "Of course."
> "Then why aren't you picketing?"
> "Popkin says you shouldn't picket. He's really out of sorts."
> "Who's Popkin?"
> "Come on. You know Popkin. He's from Guild headquarters."
> "I'm not in the Guild, I tell you." (*IT,* 215)

Some of the incidents in *The Ink Truck* suggest the Black Humor of much of the literature of the 1960s. For instance, the Guild's theme song is "Whistle While You Work," but Jarvis, the Guild's local chairman, hums it because he cannot whistle. As another example, to pass the time and to ward off Deek's sexual advances, the nurse tells Deek "hospital stories": a man bled to death on the operating table; a man had pus in his eye and waited too long to treat it; and one night "everybody forgot to give a patient anesthesia when he was operated on for throat cancer. 'We all talked about it,' the nurse said" (*IT,* 241).

The surrealism of *The Ink Truck* arises from and complements the novel's absurd world. In 1969, Kennedy said that *The Ink Truck* is an "effort to tell, in original style, a story that rides on a cushion of fetid and slightly flabby air, approximately six inches off the ground at all times."[15] In 1984, he said that *The Ink Truck* is a "willful leap into surrealism. It grew out of expressionism, out of dream, out of Kafka, Beckett, Rabelais. I can't remember whom I was reading when I wrote *The Ink Truck*—certainly all those people and dozens more, including the surrealist painters, whom I love, especially Magritte."[16] One surrealistic incident in *The Ink Truck* includes the Inferno images that mark Bailey's kidnapping by the gypsies—"Demons danced . . . faces turned into bats, bodies into flying corpses. Arms became penises with pitchfork heads. Bats turned into flying vaginas" (*IT,* 75). Other surrealistic details include Bailey's descent into the State Library's subterranean stacks; the scenes at Stanley's "house of health" where Grace Bailey, after being levitated with an electric cattle prod, crashes to the floor in a "thousand fragments, like the dusty clay of a shattered Etruscan wine jar"; and Stanley's ascent to the ceiling "like a helium balloon" where he utters "soft wolf curses that could not be understood but whose meaning could not be misread" (*IT,* 264, 265).

Regarding surrealism in *The Ink Truck,* Kennedy says he tried "to leap out of realism because I felt the whole world of Dos Passos and O'Hara, a world I once revered, was now dead to me. I couldn't do that any longer, couldn't write another realistic line. I was trying to make sense of a new age in which, for me, Kafka was far more of a prophet than anybody with realistic politics."[17] Kennedy's intention coincides with what Heller, Kesey, Vonnegut, and others were doing—rejecting realism and discovering new techniques for interpreting a contemporary world in which old values had been lost, eternal verities had to be redefined, and characters had to establish purpose and meaning in life. For Kennedy, surrealism and the absurd represent the new age and epitomize the upheavals and blurrings that occur, or, as Bailey realizes, his "steadfast illusions . . . have become far more compelling than most of my shifting realities" (*IT,* 166). The surrealistic details of Bailey's kidnapping emphasize the blurring effects that the hospital sedatives have on his mind and body, and the library section's surrealism reflects Bailey's thought processes when, as he reads the 1832 newspaper, he becomes lost in his reverie's labyrinth. While the surrealistic details of Stanley's party imply the effects of the drugged wine and food, they also emphasize the blurrings between Stanley's human and bizarre natures.

In *The Ink Truck,* the newspaper conglomerate and Stanley's devious and various tactics to end the strike epitomize Mass Society. When bargaining fails, for example, Stanley lures the more financially strained strikers with pay-raise promises, yet when they return to work and are no longer welcomed in the Guild hall, he cuts their pay. Stanley also plasters Fobie's bar and neighborhood with circulars offering an all-expenses-paid, monthlong vacation at the company-owned Florida resort, and twenty-two "winter weary strikers" accept the offer, vow to continue striking after their vacation, but rejoin company ranks. Stanley's other successful ploy is renting an office above the Guild room, staging a "series of Granny strip shows," and luring "the half dozen Guild members over sixty-five" back to the newspaper. Besides using goon squads to beat strikers, Stanley hired Queen Putzina and her gypsies to spy on strikers and even stand "sullen watches" outside their homes. Stanley's most devious tactic, however, is the orgy at his house where, under the influence of drugged food and wine, he attempts to reconcile everyone to the newspaper conglomerate:

Our mandate is clear, and it would be a simple matter for such overwhelming victors to view losers as a cargo of outcasts, that the company has no heart. But look—here we huddle in the heat of this room . . . in much the same way the caveman probably huddled beside the fire in times of storm and stress, huddled with strangers or even men he presumed yesterday to be his enemies. Reconciliation is the order of the day. Love thy neighbor, that is the call of the Christian. Joy to the world, that is the anthem of the Christs of every age. And so I offer you here tonight, my very good friends, an abundance of love, a very mountain of joy from the bottom of the company's enormous heart . . . You are all suffering . . . and I ask you to let me palliate that suffering. You are all afraid, and I ask that you let me give you courage. You are all confused, and I ask that you let me bring clarity to your days. (*IT,* 256–257)

The party's next phase takes place in Stanley's "house of health," a huge sauna where the guests disrobe while Miss Blue chants, "Flesh and skin, Stanley makes our joy begin," as Stanley stuns his guests with an electric cattle prod (*IT,* 261).

Stanley praises the company's "enormous heart" and insists that he can "palliate" their sufferings, give them courage, and bring clarity into their lives. In the topsy-turvy world of *The Ink Truck,* however, Stanley's "house of health" becomes a metaphorical death house in that the guests not only lose their dignity—shedding their clothes and being prodded by Stanley—but they will also lose their individuality as they are atomized and homogenized. In a sense, their fate is similar to that of the dissenters in *1984*—love Big Brother and die—a fate Bailey must avoid.

The 1960s Hero and Bailey: Kennedy's First Warrior

Kennedy labels his heroes "warriors" who strive to become "something valuable in life and to sustain a serious attitude toward survival."[18] While Bailey is a seminal figure for Kennedy's later heroes, he is more akin to the absurd, antiheroes of 1960s fiction. W. T. Lhamon even describes Bailey as "one of the noble zanies to whom the novels of the '60s fondly tended here and abroad."[19] As a rebel and outsider, Bailey's clothes are badges of his rebellion—a checkered sports coat, green hiplength muffler, black corduroy car coat with a fur collar, and black cossack hat—clothes that in eccentricity compare with costriker Rosenthal's black cape, swagger stick, and Tyrolean hat with its fat red feather. Moreover, their clothes recall Holden Caulfield's red hunting cap which he wears backward, McMurphy's whale underwear, and Ignatius J. Reilly's green cap, voluminous tweed trousers, and desert boots.

At the same time, because of Bailey's eccentricities and actions, Fobie's bar crowd call him a communist, "madman, idiot, jerk, creep, nut, fool and stoop. But with big balls" (*IT,* 220), epithets, however, that "changed depending on his last outrage" (*IT,* 9). When Bailey performs his "crazed gorilla" routine in front of Stanley and the news media, for example, a news commentator believes that Bailey is "probably certifiably mad" (*IT,* 242). This epithet applies also to Yossarian, McMurphy, and Holden—those radicals and rebels who, like Bailey, confront the establishment, refuse to conform, assert their individuality and who, Bailey included, underscore one 1960s theme—logic in lunacy. Kennedy even says that individualism "comes to the fore . . . when Bailey becomes the solitary striker in a year-old newspaper strike. The point is that even when the strike is taken away from him he continues to strike . . . It has become an utterly absurd pursuit by any standard except his own [and] that kind of madness is certainly going to define the individual as an eccentric, maybe a madman. You know, these extreme attitudes really create the possibilities of our existence."[20]

Like his fictional contemporaries, Bailey sees conformity as capitulation and rebels against it. Bailey's isolation and alienation are heightened when he becomes the steadfast striker because, as the novel opens, Irma is the 247th Guild defector and Rosenthal totters precariously on the brink of defection, especially after his house is trashed. Despite being clubbed and beaten by company guards and kidnapped, tortured, and cursed by the gypsies, Bailey still dreams of bleeding a company ink truck of its ink because he knows that "trouble, if it doesn't kill you, strengthens you" (*IT,* 82–83).

Bailey's physical size and strength mirror his inner fortitude. He is "built like a black bear, an ox, a rhinoceros," and Rosenthal even introduces Bailey to Deek as "our prize bull" (*IT,* 9, 36). Moreover, during the first aborted attempt to sabotage the company ink truck, Bailey charged across the company lot "like a goaded bull, head down" and "butted the back of a guard" (*IT,* 54). In operating Miss Blue's sexual toro-machine, Bailey dons a bull mask complete with horns. Even Skin says, "You won't die. You're tough. I've studied you" (*IT,* 86). Irma says Bailey is an "iceberg," a "tree with roots as deep as his leaves were tall," and refers to him as "Bailey the Jesus. Bailey the Buddha. Bailey the magician" (*IT,* 59, 139). Moreover, Bailey's strength, charmisma, and vision keep Irma and Rosenthal from defecting, and inspire Deek to join the strike.

Because of Bailey's sheer determination and his ability to inspire others, the company and Stanley agree to drop arson charges and not blacken the Guild's reputation, but only if Bailey personally apologizes to Stanley. During this meeting Bailey refuses and renews the struggle, a refusal recalling

Yossarian's refusal to cooperate with Colonels Cathcart and Korn and McMurphy's refusal to cooperate with the Big Nurse. Stanley even offers Bailey a deal: "I'm offering you a way out. A simple apology to show you're sincere, and I'll put you back to work with a fat raise. We'll all forget about the past . . . Is that cutting your heart out?" (*IT*, 121). In a heroic reaffirmation of the human will, Bailey rejects Stanley's odious compromise:

> I spit on your spit, because you don't even know anything about the Guild. You never worked twenty years to teach yourself everything there was to know about how to do a thing . . . And you never learned how . . . to be with a man and have him know you know what he's all about and get him to tell you about his life and his loves and his faults, which is the trick, to get him to tell you where he's weakest. As a con man you're a joke, Stanley. You bring me in here to con me, and you don't even know where to begin. You never learned that trick, which is the basic tool, because it's not in you and never will be and nobody can put it in you. You'll never even know how much there is to know, because the trick is untranslatable and nontransferable. (*IT*, 123)

If he were to apologize and rejoin the newspaper, Bailey would negate his past battles and lose his dignity and significance as an individual. To quote Irma, an apology would have been "the most abject humiliation in the history of Bailey" (*IT*, 125).

At this juncture, Bailey is even more isolated since Jarvis suspends him from the Guild for refusing to apologize and since he is unsure about what to do next although he realizes that his actions "were a triumph of a kind, an assertion of the unique self" (*IT*, 129). Bailey, like Kennedy's other heroes, must fall before he can rise, a fall that actually begins when the gypsies trash Rosenthal's home, Uncle Melvin will not lend Bailey two thousand dollars to help Rosenthal, and Bailey is driven "even deeper into the gloom of guilt" (*IT*, 157). Bailey's archetypal descent into the underworld occurs when he accepts a menial job with the State Library and descends into the stacks, "the burial vault of the past" located at "one of the city's deepest points" (*IT*, 157). Kennedy alludes to Bailey's eventual regeneration in this section's prefatory quotation from Joseph Campbell's *The Hero With a Thousand Faces:* "When our day is come for the victory of death, death closes in; there is nothing we can do except be crucified—and resurrected; dismembered totally, and then reborn" (*IT*, 155).

During his days in the library's lower depths, Bailey assesses his life and actions and sheds certain illusions—he is "dismembered totally and then reborn." He realizes that the Guild is an illusion, "an unreal dream that had no possibility of being realized. It was hopelessness" and a "hideous recurring death that he would die no more" (*IT,* 160). In the conversation with the Voice, Bailey also abandons "the old way of life" even though, depending on their interpretation, people may label his actions "wonderful, sad, fitting, terrible, stupid, grotesque, absurd, egocentric, hilarious and meaningless" (*IT,* 164). As the conversation between Bailey and the Voice continues, Bailey confesses that "we're all victims of our own matrix" and the "only way out is not only freedom from history, but from future glory lusting as well," and then adds: "The quality of the man, of course, dictates the achievement . . . And I do wonder about my own niche but without conclusion. All I can say is that my steadfast illusions in this time have become far more compelling than most of my shifting realities, and I'd like to take this opportunity to curse all those who have helped me reach this inverted pinnacle" (*IT,* 166). When the Voice queries Bailey about the future, Bailey says that he will move resolutely toward it even though he may perish in its blackness while he pursues the "light," follows the "dream," and clutches the "grail." When and if he encounters the black "Monster of Infinite Eyes," he will hurl his "last grenade" into the Monster's maw, ride out on the Monster's blood, and "stand bloodied up from tooth holes and digestive acids, I suppose; but if the plan works, bloody well cleansed as well. I'll stand, then, into one of those ruby days; one of those new and brilliantly ruby days; one of those arrival days. At least, that's the plan" (*IT,* 167).

These details are significant for several reasons. First, Bailey believes change is important and should be the Guild's major objective, but since the Guild has too many rules and regulations and is easily swayed by Stanley, Bailey realizes that the Guild itself represents "hopelessness" and a "hideous recurring death" that would be meaningless. Just as Yossarian finally learns that the catch-22 does not exist, Bailey tells Rosenthal and Irma, "We never needed the Guild. It was just a name we called ourselves" (*IT,* 217). Second, in the absurd world in which his illusions are "steadfast" and his realities "shifting," Bailey has indeed reached the "inverted pinnacle," a Dantean image that implies Bailey must either rise, as did Dante once he and Virgil reached Hell's pit, or remain forever fallen. Finally, Bailey's Ahab-like defiance in the face of overwhelming forces—the Monster of Infinite Eyes— affirms his belief that as long as he acts he may eventually be led into the light—"one of those arrival days."

Bailey's other surrealistic adventure in the library's stacks occurs as he reads an 1832 newspaper about Albany's cholera epidemic, loses himself in reverie, and sees pigs snuffling along the library aisles. In an attempt to escape from the pigs, Bailey sees a light and moves toward it and through a door into Albany's past and a cholera epidemic. As he roams Albany's streets he witnesses numerous absurd events. Rival fire companies fight each other as a building burns; a merchant claims that the cholera is over because an official manifesto declares it over; the City Council cancels evening church services because cholera is supposedly more deadly at night. In another incident, a preacher explains that the people's sins cause the epidemic, and Bailey exclaims, "You didn't sin . . . You're just ignorant . . . You're a madman telling these people filthy lies." (*IT,* 181). For this Bailey is clubbed on the head by a vestryman. Another absurd incident involves an alderman who preaches at an infant girl's funeral. Although two of his children still live, the alderman wishes he could die and join his dead wife and children. Next, he talks about how well made the infant's coffin is, where he procured the wood, and how the thought of worms crawling in and out of her eye sockets unnerves him. Bailey calls the alderman a "cheap quitter" for wishing to die and a madman for his remarks about the coffin and worms: "You don't say that sort of thing at a child's funeral. Is there anybody who isn't mad?" (*IT,* 183). Bailey then escapes to the immigrant village on the city's outskirts where the people gather around him, awestruck because he came there willingly. Bailey realizes, however, that the "future of this impromptu village was total doom" and that some of the villagers "would resent him . . . as some old statuary to befoul" while others "would clean off the statue, keep it shined for awe-seekers" (*IT,* 186). Bailey escapes again by moving towards a light shining through a doorway that he must kick open.

When combined with his other surrealistic fantasy with the Voice, Bailey's return to Albany's 1832 past provides insights into his dilemma. The preacher, alderman, and the others are maddened by the cholera's deadliness, and when he brings them a saving message—"Pen the pigs. Clean up your garbage"—Bailey is either ignored or clubbed. Bailey is also either ignored or beaten during the strike. In addition, just as he realized that he must hurl his "last grenade" into the monster's black maw, he also knows that to remain in the immigrant camp may mean death or at least a resignation to the order of things—"They'll either die or they won't, but they have no escape," says the young harlot (*IT,* 183). Once again Bailey seeks the light, affirming action over passiveness, life over death. In any case, Bailey is damned either way. If he refuses to resume the struggle against Stanley and the company, he will become impassive and damned; if he resumes the struggle, he will certainly be clubbed and beaten and still never succeed in bleeding the company ink truck.

Emerging from his adventures into Albany's light of day, Bailey knows he will not die and, more importantly, that "things seemed unfinished . . . He felt no rancor toward the company people or gypsies. Outrage had faded. Revenge had no foothold in him . . . I am greater. I have the final say . . . He was done with useless argument" (*IT,* 199). Just as Yossarian refused to fly more missions and McMurphy renewed the struggle against Big Nurse, Bailey renews the strike and has the "final say." Having the final say has always motivated Bailey because he "confronts the flow of life by running into the middle of it" (*IT,* 160). Moreover, while others deride his actions as hollow, insane, communistic, and absurd, Bailey understands that they are actually "triumphs of a kind, an assertion of the unique self," and so when he resumes picketing, he also begins a hunger strike as a "personal statement" (*IT,* 129, 222). Like Yossarian's and McMurphy's rebellious actions, Bailey's defiance inspires others to act, and soon Rosenthal, Irma, Deek, and ten others are again picketing.

Violence again erupts as Deek beats Smith and is in turn beaten by Fats Morelli and Clubber Reilly. At this point, Bailey sees a company ink truck, and like the lone western gunfighter walking down the street to accept a challenge, Bailey walks past "dudes and dappers," "cringers," and "professional nix-nucklers." As he begins to run toward yet another clubbing, he is, however, "conscious of more blood, more guilt, of the central core of himself that demanded sacrificial offerings, that conspired against his peace, sanity, and the sweet beauty of resignation" (*IT,* 231). He finally succeeds in bleeding the company ink truck and marking the "earth with his signature." As he is again severely beaten and falls forward, Bailey's triumph is evident in his "soundless, utterly internal but inescapably joyous giggle" (*IT,* 232).

Bailey's ultimate victory occurs during Stanley's surrealistic orgy. At first Bailey neither eats nor drinks because he knows that the drugs may force him into the party's sexual abandonment and then he would be under Stanley's influence. When Bailey views himself as some "beneficent deity: aloof, perceptive of the nature of frailty," however, he does not want to be a "sanctimonious son of a bitch" either, so he begins to eat and drink much to Stanley's delight. Although he feels the effects of the drugged food and wine, Bailey nevertheless remains aloof even during the "health phase" in Stanley's "house of health": "Bailey tried to stand motionless . . . trying to hold dominion over the spot where his feet touched the hot slats. He held his head aloft, at times on tiptoe, and became conscious of the aloofness this betrayed: a foolish faith. They cannot reach me if I don't falter" (*IT,* 262). When Stanley stuns Smith with the cattle prod, Bailey, who now suddenly feels compassion for Smith, fires Irma's ancient pistol, and he, Irma, and Smith are thrown out of the party.

As Bailey, Irma, and Rosenthal return to the now abandoned Guild room,

Bailey, who does not like unhappy endings, offers another one of his riddles: "I know the sound of one hand clapping, but what is the fruit of the fun tree?" (*IT*, 278). The "sound of one hand clapping" refers to Bailey's solitary picketing and hunger strike, but the "fruit of the fun tree" has a dual meaning: it suggests that the strike may still be fruitful, and it suggests what Bailey has endured and enjoyed about the strike. Despite the clubbings and beatings, Bailey never surrendered his dignity and individuality and will have the "final say." At the same time, the three staunchest strikers are back in the Guild room, and, in a symbolic protest, Bailey has smashed the window to gain entrance. The novel ends affirmatively because Bailey, Irma, and Rosenthal will continue to battle Stanley and the newspaper conglomerate. Significantly, the "thin, frail line of hope," a characteristic of 1960s fiction, endures in Bailey's resolution to "get on with it":

Did he really make it tough for himself to live in the world? He had never looked at the problem that way . . . So many absurd things happened to himself and others because of his response. Things bloomed or died according to how he behaved. It was unfortunate . . . He could not change everything. He had changed some things, but he could not become a different man. So what if he failed? If he hadn't failed what would he be today? Nothing but a cheap success. So the hell with it. Bolly it. Bollywolly it . . . Bolly the whole bleeding mess. Whatever was wrong, it hadn't killed him. He could still pour in the beer and pump out the syrup.
Let's get on with it," Bailey said. (*IT*, 275)

Loomings: Setting, Character, Surrealism

Although the paperback cover claims that the setting for *The Ink Truck* is a "medium-sized American city resembling Albany," in the 1984 "Preface" Kennedy writes: "All that needs saying is that this is not a book about an anonymous city, but about Albany, New York, and a few of its dynamics during two centuries." At the same time, Kennedy says, "Even though Albany is never mentioned in *The Ink Truck*, I feel I have the same streets, and the same newspaper . . . with the same characters running saloons, the same traditional figures existing in the history of this mythic city I'm inhabiting in my imagination."[21] Yet, *The Ink Truck* is usually not grouped with Kennedy's "Albany cycle" novels, probably because it does not contain the detailed, historic sense of place evident in the later novels. *Legs, Billy Phelan's Greatest Game,* and *Ironweed* contain, for example, specific references to places like the Kenmore Hotel, the Knights of Columbus hall, Clinton Square, the Christian Brothers' School, St. Agnes Cemetery; to specific

42   WILLIAM KENNEDY

streets like North Pearl, Broadway, Dove, Colonie; to specific events like the
1913 flood, the 1901 trolley strike, and the Brothers' School fire. Even
Quinn's Book, which is set in the 1850s and 1860s, refers specifically to
Albany and its history. *The Ink Truck* refers to the cholera epidemic, Goat
Hill, Cabbageville, and the newspaper that, while not specifically named as it
is in *Billy Phelan*, is Albany's *Times-Union*, but these references are not interconnected with the characters' lives and actions as they so successfully are in
the later novels. For example, in *Ironweed* as Francis rides on Rosskam's junk
wagon, he passes various places, neighborhoods, and streets that figured
prominently in Albany's past and in his own matrix. Even Bailey's return to
Albany's 1832 past, which Anne Tyler claims is "our first sense of a real place
that we can practically touch,"[22] does not connect Bailey's wanderings with
specific places. These examples aside, Kennedy's focus upon Albany as his
fictional world in *The Ink Truck* foreshadows his more detailed use of Albany
in his later novels.

After *The Ink Truck* was reissued, critics noted that Bailey presages
Kennedy's later heroes. R.Z. Sheppard writes, "With his private validity,
Bailey is a forerunner of Kennedy's Legs Diamond roaring confidently
through the twenties, gun in hand; Billy Phelan conquering Albany with
bowling ball and pool cue; and Phelan's father, Francis, a tormented bum
stripped of everything except his will to endure."[23] Similarly, Joel Conarroe
writes, "Like Legs Diamond . . . and Francis Phelan . . . he is a battler who
courts disaster, a man who knows the debauchery of the spirit that follows in-
tense failure yet who somehow survives, mired in hope. And like Billy Phelan
. . . Bailey follows a sharply defined code of conduct, believing that a man
has to do what he has to do."[24]

In relation to Kennedy's later heroes, Bailey is, however, more closely akin
to Jack Diamond in that both willfully remain outside the establishment as
rebels and outlaws—Irma even refers to Bailey as an "outlaw"—but Bailey is
a social outsider while Diamond is an actual gangster outside the law. In typical 1960s antiheroic fashion, Bailey seeks his identity and purpose outside
the establishment and society; in contrast, Daniel Quinn, Billy, and Francis
Phelan seek meaning and purpose within the confines of society, Billy by returning to Albany's Nighttime world, Francis by returning to his family, and
Daniel Quinn by embracing humanity and by marrying Maud Fallon. Yet,
all of Kennedy's heroes live by a definite code as typified by Francis in
Ironweed: "The trick was to live, to beat the bastards, survive the mob and the
fateful chaos, and show them all what a man can do to set things right, once
he sets his mind to it."[25] Bailey survives the mob and the fateful chaos of his
own doubts and foibles by trusting himself and his inner promptings. The

"inverted pinnacle" from which he must rise or remain fallen parallels Billy Phelan's fall from McCall grace, Francis Phelan's bumdom, and Daniel Quinn's descent into the Civil War's "mudholes of Hell."

Although Kennedy says the *The Ink Truck* is a "willful leap into surrealism," he abandoned surrealism in his later novels: "I felt I couldn't go on writing this hyperbolic comedy which is always six inches off the ground. I needed to be grounded in reality. *Legs* is a consequence of that."[26] After initially writing *Legs* as pure myth and learning that the plot was "still too far off the ground," Kennedy then realized that the "myth had to grow out of the real, otherwise I wasn't writing from substance but was inventing lifeless metaphors that didn't say anything interesting about gangsters or anything else either . . . So I was working for authenticity of a kind in *Legs,* and *Billy Phelan* is an obvious extension of that."[27]

Although *The Ink Truck* was Kennedy's first novel and not as well received as his later works, Kennedy did precisely what he said he was going to do—he wrote about the 1960s. As a book about this turbulent decade, *The Ink Truck* is just as chilling as *One Flew Over the Cuckoo's Nest,* just as absurd as *Catch-22,* and just as experimental in its techniques as any of the avant-garde works of the era.

Chapter Four
"Products of One Man's Imagination": *Legs*

Although the first reviews of William Kennedy's *Legs* were generally more favorable than those about *The Ink Truck,* Bruce Allen faults the novel because Kennedy never criticized or questioned Marcus Gorman's "mindless life-force worship" of Legs Diamond, and Allen concludes his review by claiming that *Legs* is a "made-for-TV book" and so people should consult their "local listings for time and station."[1] On the other hand, while stating that *Legs* is a "good book but not a great one," L. J. Davis concludes, "*Legs* is what a novel is supposed to be: a mirror walking down the road of man, and it deserves our closest and most serious attention."[2] In reviewing Michael Crichton's *The Great Train Robbery,* James Crumley's *The Wrong Case,* and Kennedy's *Legs,* all of which he labels "crime fiction" novels, Peter S. Prescott writes that *Legs* is the "most substantial of the lot, not a crime novel at all but a real novel about a criminal—there is a difference. Kennedy means to probe our peculiar American habit of reviling gangsters while pressing them for autographs."[3] Prescott's distinction between a "crime novel" and a "real novel about a criminal" may not be clear, but his observation is significant because Kennedy explains America's fascination with Diamond in *Legs.*

As they did with *The Ink Truck,* later reviewers, aided by retrospective comparisons, evaluate *Legs* in terms of its place in Kennedy's writings. Loxley F. Nichols criticizes its "inconsequential details and innumerable dimly defined characters" but notes: "Albany not only gives Kennedy place, but it also gives him subject, and through subject he acquires time, the 1930s, a period to which he has adhered in his last two novels."[4] Dean Flower thinks, however, that *Legs* is Kennedy's best novel and that *Billy Phelan's Greatest Game* is "almost as good" because "both reek of city room slang, love of fact, bottom-line bluntness, and headline speed," and then Flower adds: "*Legs* is a shade more convincing, not because Kennedy dramatizes an historic figure . . . but because he is created for us by Marcus Gorman and because Gorman pieces the story together from memories. Twice distanced, the speakeasies and gangsters and fast talk seem immediate and legendary with Irish-

Catholic Albany as a microcosm of the thirties."[5] Anne Mills King argues that *Legs* is "tightly crafted, with parallel scenes, apt literary allusions, well-constructed flashbacks, foreshadowing throughout, and, always, the map of Albany and its neighboring Catskills in mind."[6]

That Marcus Gorman's "life-force worship" is mindless (Gorman is aware of his own moral lapses), that *Legs* is a book made for TV (its plot and characterizations are too multilayered for television), and that, as Flower believes, it is Kennedy's best novel are matters of opinion and therefore arguable. Still, *Legs* is indeed a gangster novel, but not in the classic sense that George Grella establishes in "The Gangster Novel: The Urban Pastoral." At the same time, in comparison with *The Ink Truck*, *Legs* is more tightly structured, contains a more detailed sense of place, and foreshadows Kennedy's later novels while also denoting a maturing of Kennedy's literary techniques.

Kennedy on *Legs*

Regarding *Legs*, Kennedy says, "When I started to write that book it was not about Legs Diamond. He was just going to be a character. And I looked at our morgue at the paper. Holy Christ! The things that had happened to him."[7] Kennedy's initial introduction to and fascination with Diamond's career and life propelled him on a "maniacal quest for background" during which he spent "a small fortune xeroxing newspapers."[8] Initially, Kennedy wanted *Legs* to be "historical in outline," and a "meticulously documented piece of fiction," but after discovering numerous contradictory accounts in newspapers and magazines about Diamond's life, Kennedy finally decided to "reinvent" Diamond as a "brand-new fictional character," and thus while *Legs* is historically factual, "the daily specifics of Jack, his wife, Alice, and his girlfriend Marion (Kiki) Roberts, and his gangland cronies and enemies are products of one man's imagination" (*OA*, 200). At any rate, Kennedy says, "It's the last time I ever intended to research a novel. Too much research can overburden the imagination."[9]

Although Kennedy claims that he never intended to write a trilogy about Albany when he wrote *Legs*,[10] he admits that he chose Diamond because of the gangster's Albany ties. Besides being a rumrunner and bootlegger who supplied Albany's speakeasies, Diamond had mob dealings with Albany's Oley brothers. More specifically, Diamond not only recuperated at Albany Hospital after the Aratoga Inn assassination attempt, but he partied at O'Brien's Parody Club on Hudson Avenue and at the Kenmore Hotel's Rain-Bo Room while he awaited trial for kidnapping Grover Parks (in *Legs* Grover Parks becomes Clem Streeter), a trial for which Diamond hired

Daniel H. Prior, Albany's preeminent criminal lawyer. In addition, while keeping Kiki Roberts in an apartment at 21 Ten Broeck Street, Diamond moved Alice and his dead brother's wife, Kitty, and nephew, Johnny, into Mrs. Laura Woods's rooming house at 67 Dove Street—"all part of Jack's humanizing entourage during the Troy Trial" (*OA*, 205). Diamond's last and eternal Albany tie occurred when unknown assailants murdered him in the Dove Street rooming house after his acquittal party at Freddie Young's speakeasy, which in *Legs* becomes the Parody Club.

Kennedy also chose Jack Diamond as a fictional character because he personified the age: "I chose Legs because he was a character who had galvanized the imagination of America. Legs is another version of the American dream—that you can grow up and shoot your way to fame and fortune."[11] Because Kennedy decided to use "everything: the truth, the lies, the legends, the myths" about Diamond, *Legs* becomes, to quote Kennedy, "a journalistic report, not on gangsters, but on the way America looks at gangsters."[12] Kennedy's fictional portrait, however, also reveals Diamond's human side because, according to Kennedy, "I don't think of gangsters as animals beyond redemption, or inarticulate, or that they have no soul . . . The people that live this kind of life are human beings like you and me. People did love Legs Diamond."[13] Kennedy's portrait of Diamond as a human being, gangster, and an historical and mythical figure gives *Legs* its depth and power.

Diamond Facets

In "The Death of Legs Diamond" from *O Albany!*, Kennedy declares that Diamond's "cruelty pervades my book" and that even Kiki Roberts said that Diamond "was meaner than most people realized, that he didn't mind torturing and shooting people" (*OA*, 200). In referring to Diamond's gangster personality and the purpose of *Legs*, Kennedy says that "to write about Diamond I had to respect someone who was a mean, cruel son-of-a-bitch . . . My role was to find out why he was so revered . . . Why people courted his presence."[14]

As Kennedy presents it in *Legs*, Diamond's life was interwoven with violence and death. Diamond is almost assassinated four times, and the killings he either commits or orders are just as violently cruel. In the Hotsy Totsy Club shootout that opens the novel's main action, for example, an enraged Diamond fires one shot into Tim Reagan's stomach, three into his head, two into his groin, pulls the trigger on empty chambers, and then cracks Billy Reagan on the head with the empty pistol. Early in his career when he is working for Arnold Rothstein, Diamond murders Wilson, a card-playing cheat, even though Rothstein does not specifically order Wilson's death. As Diamond explains to Gorman: "I took him to the river with a driver and walked him to the edge of a dock. He offered me four grand, all he had left from the game, and I took it. Then I shot him three times and dumped him in. It turned out he had three kids . . . Maybe I wouldn't have killed him if he didn't say that about the haircut, make me feel I was such a bum . . . With four grand I wasn't a bum anymore. I bought a new suit and got a haircut at the Waldorf-Astoria" (*L,* 95).

After being nearly assassinated, Diamond has Ace O'Hagan murdered, and Diamond shoots the trigger man, Billy Blue, three times in the stomach and then calmly watches as Murray "The Goose" Pucinski, a Diamond henchman, jabs an ice pick "a half dozen times" into each of Blue's temples. In another revenge killing, Diamond burns Red Moran up in an automobile, and because Moran's girlfriend can identify Diamond, he ties her feet to a sewer grate and throws her into the river. Because Jimmy Biondo threatened Kiki Roberts, Tony "The Boy" Amapola, a Biondo muscleman, is shot "through the head and neck four times and dumped outside Hackensack" (*L,* 132). On Diamond's orders, Charlie Northrup, who ridiculed Diamond's dancing with Kiki and who turned informer, is severely beaten, accidentally killed, and then dismembered and burned in Diamond's still. The press aptly labels Diamond the "King Cobra of the Catskills," a title that Kennedy underscores not only by the references to sudden violence in Diamond's life, but also by describing Diamond's eyes in the Weissberg scene: Diamond's "eyes turned snakish, with a grimace of hate and viciousness," eyes Flossie says "that looked right through doors and walls" (*L,* 110–11, 101).

In depicting Legs Diamond as a bootlegger, hijacker ("one of the pioneers in this field," writes Kennedy in *O Albany!*), mob boss, and cold-blooded killer, *Legs* belongs, in one sense, to the gangster novel tradition. George Grella claims that W. R. Burnett's *Little Caesar* (1929) "turned the gangster novel into a powerful and influential type" and "remains the classic gangster story."[15] Furthermore, in characterizing Caesar "Rico" Bandello, the novel's protagonist, Grella describes him as a "tough guy in his purest form" and "without antecedents, relationships, ties of any important kind; a man devoid of love and almost without lust; a gunman who kills without hate or remorse; an Italian with no Italian qualities; a gang leader who cares for none of the rewards of leadership except the sense of power" and who "inspired all the imitations of the gunmen who proliferate in fiction, motion pictures, and television programs."[16] Diamond is also a "tough guy" in his language and posturings, relishes his own sense of power, lives outside of the law, inspires fear—"Jack's strong suit was menace" (L, 104)—and kills readily and often. On the other hand, in portraying Diamond's human side, Kennedy not only adds a new dimension to the gangster novel tradition, but uses Diamond's personality to explain the public's fascination with this public enemy. To quote Kennedy, "I was convinced that my mission in Legs was to write a meticulously accurate historical gangster novel. Then I found out that the mission was not possible. There was no such animal. It could never be done because of conflicting stories."[17]

In Legs, some of the conflicting stories humanize Diamond. Saul Baker, the Hotsy Totsy Club doorman, had been paroled from Sing Sing when Diamond offers him a job—"Don't try to tell Saul Baker Jack Diamond was a heartless man" (L, 121). In other instances, Diamond donates money for a new organ at Sacred Heart Church in Cairo, New York, pays to have an old woman's shed rebuilt, and pays the ambulance and the Albany Hospital bill for an older couple's son—"People in Acra and Catskill told these stories when the papers said Jack was a heartless man" (L, 52). Although Diamond's motives are mercenary, he hires Jesse Franklin to operate an applejack still "at a hundred a week, a pay raise of about eight hundred percent" (L, 38). The passengers on board the Belgenland want his picture and autograph and assure Diamond that "they didn't believe such a nice person as he would have anything to do with such goings on" (L, 82).

Other humanizing anomalies include Diamond's carrying a rosary, attending Sunday Mass, and even believing that he has not been gunned down because he is in "God's grace . . . God wants me to live" (L, 163). In addition, Gorman describes Diamond in purely human terms as Diamond recovers from the Monticello Hotel assassination attempt: his lips quiver as he sleeps, his ears stick out, his "eyes were separated by a vertical furrow of care just above the nose," and he "wheezed just like other Americans in their sleep" (L, 162). Kiki describes his scarred body resulting from his violent life, and Alice talks about the twenty-five "squiggles" signifying the number of times she and Diamond made love on their weekend honeymoon in Atlantic City. In another scene, Gorman highlights Diamond's human side: "I'd been watching Jack have fun all day, first with his machine gun and then his champagne and his Rabelais and his dream of a purple mansion" (L, 56).

Interspersed throughout the narrative are dramatic scene shifts between everyday life and sudden or potential violence, scenes that underscore Diamond's conflicting human and cobra-deadly personalities. One of the most compelling and technically perfect scenes occurs, for instance, at Mike Brady's Top O' the Mountain House at Haines Fall where Diamond meets Kiki Roberts. After insisting on buying Gorman a glass paperweight souvenir—another humanizing incident: "Forty–nine cents. The action was outrageously sentimental" (*L, 57*)—Diamond, Gorman, and Joe "Speed" Fogarty enter Brady's where stands Charlie Northrup, a "physical power, about six four and two forty," who had once been in the same gang with Diamond but who now has refused to meet with him. Incensed, Diamond menacingly reminds Northrup of another meeting, "Charlie, old brother, don't have me send for you" (*L, 57*). Immediately after this taut encounter, Diamond dances with Kiki in a scene that Gorman describes in humanizing terms:

"C'mon, Jackie," said Kiki, her breasts in fascinating upheaval. Jack looked at her and his feet began to move, left out, right kick, right back, left back, basic guarded, small-dimensioned movements, and then, "C'mon, dance," Kiki urged, and he gave up his consciousness of the crowd and then left out, right kick, right back, left back expanded, vitalized, and he was dancing, arms swinging, dancing, Jack Diamond, who seemed to do everything well, was dancing the Charleston and Black Bottom, dancing them perfectly, the way all America had always wanted to be able to dance them—energetically, controlled, as professionally graceful as his partner who had danced these dances for money in Broadway shows, who had danced them for Ziegfeld; and now she was dancing on the mountaintop with the king of the mountain, and they were king and queen of motion together, fluid with Fogarty's melody and beat. (*L, 60–61*)

Both the mood and the spell shatter when Charlie Northrup begins laughing and says, "Dancin' . . . the big man's dancin' . . . dancin' the Charleston on Sunday afternoon" (*L, 61*). Diamond escorts Kiki back to their table, threatens Northrup in a low voice, and walks away as Northrup spits a mouthful of beer at Diamond's back—"Not hitting him, or meaning to, but spitting as a child spits when he can think of no words as venomous as his saliva" (*L, 62*). Gorman's thoughts emphasize Diamond's gangster personality: "Holy Flying Christ, I said to myself when I understood Charlie's laughter and saw the arc of beer, for I understood much more than what we were seeing. I was remembering what Jack's stylized violence could do to a man, remembering Joe Bignola, my client in the Hotsy Totsy case, a man not visited by Jack's vengeance but merely by the specter of it" (*L, 62*).

In this scene, Kennedy juxtaposes the tough guy language and posturings with Diamond's energetic, controlled, and graceful dancing, which is not only part of his human side, but which also, as evident in Gorman's description and highlighted by Northrup's comment, becomes another facet of Diamond's life that Gorman had not expected. Moreover, other scenes in

Legs contrast the two sides of Diamond's personality. For example, as "Goose" Pucinski sits outside the Parody Club waiting to murder him, Diamond harmonizes to "My Mother's Rosary" with Flossie, Milligan, and Packy. In another incident, after dining at the Catskill's New York Restaurant, Diamond and Kiki are driving through a beautiful moonlit night holding hands when Diamond's gangster personality erupts as Clem Streeter's truck appears, and Diamond kidnaps and tortures Streeter, an act that will inevitably topple Diamond and his empire.

Besides emphasizing Legs Diamond's two personalities, the alternating scenes coincide with Marcus Gorman's observations about the balance in Diamond's life. Gorman describes, for instance, Fogarty as the "good guy" and Goose as the killer: "I no longer think it strange that Jack had both kinds—Fogarty kind, Murray kind—working for him. Jack lived a long time, for Jack, and I credit it to his sense of balance, even in violent matters, even in choices of killers and drivers, his sense that all ranges of the self must be appeased, and yet only appeased, not indulged" (*L*, 191). When Lew Edwards attempts to persuade Diamond to become an evangelist, Gorman notes Diamond's "delicate, supremely honest balancing act that would bring his life together" (*L*, 191). Diamond lives on the edge of both worlds, as is emphasized in his relationships with Alice and Kiki, or, as Gorman says: "I'd expected him to emphasize one or the other woman when he arrived, depending on his mood: horny or homey. But he balanced them neatly, emphasizing neither, impatient to see them both, moving neither away from one nor toward the other but rather toting one on each shoulder . . . which would offer instead the more beautiful alternative of both" (*L*, 121). And, according to Gorman, Diamond's final trouble began when "he stopped functioning in balance" (*L*, 137).

Diamond Technicalities

Kennedy wrote *Legs* eight different times because he tried various techniques for telling the story and finally decided to use Marcus Gorman as a narrator:

I wrote it over a period of about six years and it never worked until the final version. It worked up to a point, but I never was very satisfied. It started out as a kind of novel being written about a movie being made about this mythological hero, or antihero, and I found that to be contrived. It was a bad gimmick. The cameraman kept getting in the way of the story. Then I tried to tell it as a surrealistic work to the point that it was mystical, and that didn't work. I tried to tell it chronologically from the very earliest days, an accumulation of voices connected into a narrative and that didn't work. I tried to tell it totally through the last day of his life, the trial, and his farewell party, and that didn't work, and so on. Finally, I focused on a way of telling it. Marcus Gorman became the narrator and that was necessary. I found out that I could not have all the multiple voices and make it work. I had to have somebody collating all this. Maybe Henry James turned me around. I was reading his marvelous prefaces and notes on the novel and he was talking about the importance of an intelligent narrator and I realized that was what I needed. So I began. It just fell into place then and I also found a dramatic focus to build to a climax of his life which was the torturing of the trucker, Clem Streeter.[18]

Although Marcus Gorman's characterization has parallels in the life of Daniel H. Prior, Albany's famous criminal lawyer, Kennedy did not want Marcus "associated directly with any specific individual" and so "created a private life for Marcus which would in no way invade the private life of any lawyer I knew, actually or historically."[19]

Regarding the parallels between *Legs* and *The Great Gatsby,* especially in terms of the narrators, Kennedy admits that Diamond never met F. Scott Fitzgerald and that although "*Gatsby* was a conscious model," Gorman is different from Nick Carraway in that Nick is a "smart but boring presence . . . mainly because he rarely *does* anything":

The only time he's interesting is when he gets drunk at that hotel scene and suddenly he's outside himself, almost as if he's no longer the narrator. It's what Percy Lubbock says about James pulling back from the center of consciousness to fall silent except for the description of action; and when the action does take place you discover that the character has become visible in a different way. That's what I sought to do with Marcus—have him act and react, be the person who's subtly and slowly corrupted, into the fallen figure he becomes in addition to being the contemplative narrator who can put Diamond into a social and moral perspective.[20]

From a technical standpoint, then, Marcus Gorman not only illustrates the point of the novel's epigraph from Eugene Ionesco—"People like killers. And if one feels sympathy for the victims it's by way of thanking them for letting themselves be killed"—but as a lawyer represents a moral perspective superior to that of such other admirers as Packy Delaney, Tipper Kelley, Sal of the Kenmore, and even Alice and Kiki. Moreover, since *Legs* is also about Gorman's moral lapse that results from his fascination with Diamond, Gorman's fall provides an added dimension to the novel's plot.

Initially, Gorman becomes involved with Diamond when he accepts Diamond's offer of six quarts of Scotch in exchange for an Albany County pistol permit. Gorman accepts the Sunday dinner invitation, however, because he realizes that his life is a "stupendous bore" and "could use a little Gargantuan dimension" and he self-righteously adds that he would listen to "whatever that strange and vicious charmer had to say to an Albany barrister" (*L*, 16). Gorman is impressed, however, with Diamond's luxurious green and gray Cadillac and then further charmed by Diamond's sense of humor and the kinetic energy that makes Diamond "alive" in a way that Gorman is not. Moreover, before he target practices with a machine gun aimed at Dutch Schultz's caricature, Gorman understands the difference between his own social and moral world and what the machine gun and Diamond represent: "What a long distance between Marcus and Jack Diamond. Milleniums of psychology, civilization, experience, turpitude . . . Would I defend him if some shooters walked through the barn door? What difference from defending him in court? And what of Jack's right to justice, freedom, life? Is the form of defense the only differentiating factor? What a morally confounded fellow Marcus is, perplexed by Mr. Thompson's invention" (*L*, 40). Once he pulls the trigger, however, Gorman enjoys it, and when Diamond reaches for the weapon Gorman fires it again, "facing the ease with which I had become new. Do something new and you are new. How boring it is not to fire machine guns" (*L*, 41). Energized by this new experience with the machine gun, Gorman realizes that he is now friends with and "intuitively in sympathy" with Alice and Diamond, and when Fogarty mentions that Dutch Schultz had killed one of his cousins, Gorman rationalizes, "And so I had moral support for my little moral collapse—which sent a thrill through me, made me comfortable again on this glorious Sunday in the mountains" (*L*, 41).

Gorman's further involvement and moral collapse occur when he sails to Europe with Diamond "against all sane judgment," and especially when he agrees to wear Diamond's money belt containing Jimmy Biondo's money. Gorman recalls, "I remember my own excitement, the surge of energy I felt rising in myself from some arcane storage area of the psyche when I strapped on the money belt. No longer the voyeur at the conspiracy, I was now an accessory, and the consequence was intoxicating. I felt the need to drink, to further loosen my control center, and I did" (*L*, 106). Gorman's control collapses further when he meets a woman in the ship's bar, coaxes her back to his cabin, and subjects her to what he later calls a "quasi-rape" (*L*, 122). He lapses further when he fabricates a new identity for Jesse Franklin and when he visits Kiki: "I had no pressing business in New York, but I made it a point to go, and I presume it was for the same reason I'd helped old Jesse . . . because I was now addicted to entering the world of Jack Diamond as fully as possible. I was unable not to stick around and see how it all turned out. And, yes, I know, even as a spectator, I was condoning the worst sort of behavior. Absolute worst. I know, I know" (*L*, 143). Gorman's moral disintegration is complete when he arranges for fifteen witnesses to testify in Diamond's behalf during the first Troy trial and when he concocts the story about the nun during the second Troy trial.

Gorman's fascination with Diamond parallels Kiki's and Alice's. Just as Gorman realizes that his life needs some Gargantuan dimensions, Kiki says that when she met Diamond her "life started going someplace, someplace weird and good" (*L*, 144). Despite her Catholic heritage, Alice confesses, "Don't tell me I should've married somebody pure and holy. They would have bored the ass off me years ago" (*L*, 178). Gorman clearly recognizes the evil inherent in Diamond's life, and so do Kiki and Alice. Kiki willingly courts evil without approving of it, and Alice knows that she is "married to one of the rottenest sons of bitches to come along in this century," that he is a "crook all the way through to the dirty underwear of his psyche," and that her love for Diamond is "evidence of her moral bankruptcy" (*L*, 179, 190). In addition, neither Alice nor Kiki can desert Diamond. Alice moves to a Manhattan apartment after the first Troy trial only to return for the second Troy trial as part of Diamond's "humanizing entourage." Kiki knows that despite the "torture he did and the killing he did" she could not desert him because she wants "it all out of life . . . the most, the greatest, the flashiest, the best, the biggest, the wildest, the craziest, the worst" (*L*, 152–153). Fogarty even thinks of deserting Diamond, and after the Europe trip so does Gorman, but Gorman says, "The wiping away of my political future . . . the prospect of assassination, and my excursion into quasi-rape convinced me my life had changed in startling ways I wouldn't yet say I regretted" (*L*, 122).

Kiki, Alice, and Gorman also benefit from their associations with Diamond. After his death, both Kiki and Alice tour the theater circuits billed respectively as "See Kiki, The Gangster's Gal" and "Beautiful Mrs. Jack Legs Diamond in Person" (*L*, 301, 303). Although Gorman's law practice flourishes because of the acquittals in the Streeter cases, Gorman is fortunate in that from his privileged glimpses into the evil surrounding Diamond, he can rationalize about his Albany friends who have nixed his congressional aspirations: "What I learned from Jack was that politicians imitated his style without comprehending it, without understanding that their venality was only hypocritical. Jack failed thoroughly as a hypocrite. He was a liar, of course, a perjurer, all of that, but he was also a venal man of integrity, for he never ceased to renew his vulnerability to punishment, death, and damnation. It is one thing to be corrupt. It is another to behave in a psychologically responsible way toward your own evil" (*L*, 117–18).

Kiki's, Alice's, and especially Gorman's fascination for Diamond represents what Kennedy labels as the public's "fascination with abomination—with Bonnie and Clyde, the Godfather, Cagney and Bogart."[21] Kiki says, for instance, "We go out, me and Jack, out to the best places with the best people, rich people, I mean, society people, famous people like politicians and actors and they fall all over us . . . They want to make sex with us and kiss us and love us" (L, 144). Gorman notes a similar fascination on the European voyage:

I observed him from a distance, seeing people go out of their way for a look at him playing cards in his shirt sleeves. I saw a blond librarian ask him to dance and begin a thing with him. He was a bootlegger and, as such, had celebrity status, plus permission from the social order to kill, maim, and befoul the legal system, for wasn't he performing a social mission for the masses? The system would stay healthy by having life both ways; first relishing Jack's achievement while it served a function, then slavering sensually when his head, no longer necessary, rolled. (L, 85)

Typifying the public's admiration of Diamond is the *Hanover* sailor's comment: "A strange man, *der Schack, und* I like him . . . Good company, many stories, full of the blood that makes a man come to life as thousands around him become dead. A natural man" (L, 113).

Kennedy writes in *O Albany!* that Diamond was a "complex figure, and the world's response to him was equally complex" (OA, 199). In reinventing Diamond's life and career in *Legs*, Kennedy increases the plot's layers and Diamond's mystique by dealing with other responses to Diamond, to what the Philadelphia judge who bans him from the city terms the "twin aberrations of the public mind" (L, 120). The range of complex responses to Jack is evident in the letters he receives while recovering from the Monticello Hotel shooting. A few were hope-you-die-soon sentiments, some requested money before he dies, a majority were get-well wishes, but some were bizarre. One kind-hearted woman wanted him to drown her six kittens; a mother offers him "up to fifty-five dollars" to murder her ungrateful son; a man wants Diamond to murder him in his marble bathtub by firing "several small-caliber bullets into my anus at no quicker than thirty-second intervals"; and a woman promises to "romp" Diamond back to health as he makes love to her "on the dining room table, then in the bathroom on our new green seat, and a third time (I know you will be able to dominate me thrice) on my husband's side of the bed" (L, 161). These letters, Diamond's own revelations, and the stories about him by various people including Alice, Kiki, and Gorman, all contribute to the Diamond myth which is an integral part of the novel's structure.

Structuring the Diamond Myth

Chronologically, *Legs* focuses on Jack Diamond's career after the 1929 Hotsy Totsy Club shootout until his murder in 1931. Gorman has Sunday dinner with Diamond in midsummer, 1930, and five days later sails with him to Europe. After returning to the United States, Diamond is gunned down in the Monticello Hotel, spends two and a half months recovering in New York's Polyclinic Hospital, and is discharged on New Year's Day, 1931. In mid-April of that year, Diamond kidnaps Clem Streeter and Dickie Bartlett, and eight days later Governor Franklin Delano Roosevelt uses his executive power to bring Diamond to trial. The first Troy trial ends in an acquittal in early July, and the second Troy trial ends in an acquittal on 17 December 1931. On 18 December 1931 at about five-thirty in the morning, Diamond is murdered in the Dove Street rooming house. Within this narrowly focused chronology, however, Kennedy fleshes out Diamond's life and career with selected flashbacks that range from 1909 when Jack and Eddie, his brother, play in the abandoned Philadelphia warehouse to 1925 when Diamond begins working for Rothstein and on to 1927 when the Lepke mob tries to kill him.

Within the novel's focused chronology, these flashbacks combine with other plot details and create Legs Diamond's mythical dimensions. *Legs* even begins in myth forty-three years after Diamond's death as Tipper Kelley, Flossie, Packy Delaney, and Gorman meet in the Rain-Bo Room that, like Diamond, had its glory days in the 1920s and 1930s and where, says Gorman, "if Jack's ghost walked anywhere, it was in that bar" (*L*, 14). As these four reminisce, each relates legendary tales about Diamond. Delaney claims that Diamond had been shot thirty-nine times by two gunmen who had seven guns between them; Kelley claims that Diamond had a bull terrier named Clancy that could "toe dance"; and Flossie claims that "Jack could turn on electric lights sometimes, just by snapping his fingers" and "could run right up the wall and halfway across the ceiling when he got a good running start" (*L*, 311). *Legs* also ends in myth as Diamond visualizes a death in which his soul "disappeared into the void, into the darkness where the white was still elusive" (*L*, 317). As Kennedy remarks, "The whole thrust of the last scene had to do with Legs being reborn into this life as legend, then a mythic figure, a figure in American history who will be with us a long time to come . . . That's one of the things I was driving at in *Legs,* that sense of the gangster as myth, the idea that Legs was moving into mythic status after his life on earth."[22]

Myths usually record the passing of an era. Kennedy emphasizes the creation of Diamond's myth by concentrating on Diamond's fall and the collapse of his empire, both of which mirror the fading of the gangster era. As Gorman notes, "Coll was in jail, [Jack's] mob busted up after a shoot-out in Averill Park and a roundup in Manhattan . . . So many dead and gone. Mike Sullivan, Fatty Walsh, Eddie . . . remembering all the old boys, friends and enemies. Brocco. Babe. Frenchy. Shorty. Pretty. Mattie. Hymie. Fogarty. Dead, gone off, or in jail. And he seemed to himself, for the first time, a curiously perishable item among many such items, a thing of just so many seasons" (L, 298).

For the plot's 1929 to 1931 sequences, Kennedy selects those details that signify Diamond's fall. Diamond's career begins to wane, for instance, with the Hotsy Totsy Club shootout: "The crest of his life collapsed with the Hotsy shooting. All he'd been building to for most of the decade—his beer and booze operations, the labor racketeering, . . . his protection of crooked bucketshops, . . . his connections with the dope market, and . . . his abstract aspiration to the leadership mantle that would somehow simulate Rothstein's" (L, 67). Other plot details chronicle Diamond's fading career. Charlie Northrup spits beer at him; Diamond is barred from Europe and Philadelphia; Gorman cannot bribe Warren Van Dusen on Diamond's behalf; and Roosevelt wants Diamond tried and imprisoned. Other incidents include Brady's throwing Fogarty out of the Top O' the Mountain bar— "You and none of your bunch are welcome here. We're all through kissing your ass" (L, 218)—and Diamond's having to deliver his own bootleg whiskey to Packy Delaney—"But the pickup and delivery of the moment would be a departure for Jack: made in a borrowed truck by the man himself, notable status reduction" (L, 256). Finally, each assassination attempt takes its physical and mental toll, especially the Aratoga Inn attempt: "He was frail, down eighteen pounds again, eyes abulge again, cheekbones prominent again, left arm all but limp, and periodically wincing when he felt that double-ought pellet bobbling about in his liver. But more troubling than this was the diminishing amount of time left for him to carry out the task at hand: the balancing of the forces of his life in a way that would give him ease, let him think well of himself, show him the completion of a pattern that at least would look *something* like the one he devised as a young man" (L, 235).

As Diamond's career collapses, his mythical dimensions increase. On the European voyage, for instance, American and foreign presses "enshrined" him by giving him the same celebrity status as that of "royalty, heroes, and movie stars," inventing stories and crimes, "embellishing his history, humanizing him," and thus "taking Jack Diamond away from himself, of making him a product of the collective imagination" (*L,* 89). The German press even give him a mythic nickname, "*der Schack,*" and the British call him "Cunning Jackie."

Diamond's myth grows with the unsuccessful attempts to kill him. When he survives the Monticello attempt, he becomes "more famous than ever." The *News* and the *Mirror* have series about him and even about Kiki's memoirs, and "she and Jack were Pyramus and Thisbe for the world and no breakfast table was without them for a month" (*L,* 159). In a *Daily News* interview toward the end of his life, Diamond says he must defend himself "against the mythical crimes of the mythical Legs" (*L,* 243). The newspaper stories, those stories related by fellow gangsters and acquaintances, and especially those told by Flossie, Packy, and Tipper, all create the Diamond myth. Moreover, although Diamond is dead, Alice is murdered, and Kiki fades from headlines into history, Gorman insists, "This isn't the end of the story, of course. Didn't I, like everybody else who knew him, end up on a barstool telling Jack's tale again, forty-three years later, telling it my own way? And weren't Tipper and the Pack and Flossie there with me, ready, as always with the ear, ready to dredge up yet another story of their own?" (*L,* 309).

Through the narrative's sequences and flashbacks, then, Diamond becomes the legend suggested by the novel's last section, "Jacked Up." Moreover, in the novel's opening section, Gorman alludes to the mythical image that would transcend that "final historical image"—Diamond's corpse "clad in underwear, flat-assed out in bed, broke and alone":

I had come to see Jack as not merely the dude of all gangsters, the most active brain in the New York underworld, but as one of the truly new American Irishmen of his day: Horatio Alger out of Finn McCool and Jesse James, shaping the dream that you could grow up in America and shoot your way to glory and riches. I've said it again and again to my friends who question the ethics of this somewhat unorthodox memoir: "If you like Carnegie and Custer, you'll love Diamond." He was almost as famous as Lindbergh while his light burned. "The Most Picturesque Racketeer in the Underworld," the New York *American* called him; "Most Publicized of Public Enemies," said the *Post;* "Most Shot-At Man in America," said the *Mirror . . .* Why he was a pioneer, the founder of the first truly modern gang, the dauphin of the town for years . . . He helped kick the gong around, Jack did. (*L,* 13)

In a *New York Times* article about Diamond's death, Meyer Berger underscores the myth by referring to Diamond as the "human ammunition dump for the underworld."[23] Or, as Kennedy emphasizes, the "notion of myth . . . became central to the final version of the book; the idea of how myth is created: an act which becomes a public fascination, and then is blown out of all proportion, so that the doer is given legendary status; then the legend is passed on, and becomes one of the defining myths of the age."[24]

Legs: Backwards and Forwards—Setting and Character

Because Kennedy uses Diamond's Albany years, 1930 to 1931, as the major framework for his narrative and chooses Gorman as the narrator, *Legs* contains a more detailed sense of place than does *The Ink Truck.* Gorman opens his narrative in the Rain-Bo Room and also mentions that he waited at the Knights of Columbus hall overlooking Clinton Square before boarding a train at Union Station to meet Diamond for Sunday dinner. In another scene, Gorman meets Diamond at the Albany Elks Club, accompanies him on a bootleg delivery to Packy Delaney, and on the trip to Troy passes by specific Albany landmarks with Legs—"up Broadway and through North Albany, past the streets in my own neighborhood: Emmett, Albany, Mohawk, Genesee, Erie, then the park in front of Sacred Heart Church on Walter and North Second Streets" (*L,* 257). The purely fictional Gorman and the quasi-fictional Diamond frequent specific places in Albany thereby adding verisimilitude to Kennedy's historical fiction.

The interconnections among *Legs, Billy Phelan's Greatest Game, Ironweed,* and *Quinn's Book* contribute to the sense of place. "*Legs* was 1931, and that was researched to discover that era. And once I discovered the twenties and Prohibition and the gangland world, I began to see that it had tentacles that went forward, that people I was writing about in *Legs* were going to be significant in future books I wanted to write."[25] In *Billy Phelan's Greatest Game,* for example, Angie Velez stays at the Kenmore; Billy Phelan thinks about stopping by The Parody Club; George Quinn and Morrie Berman each tell a story about Diamond—the stories and legend continue; Hubert Maloy is one of Charlie McCall's kidnappers; and Emory Jones thinks McCall's kidnapping will be bigger news than Diamond's death. In addition, both Diamond and Marcus Gorman have been barred from Becker's, an action reminiscent of Fogarty's being barred from Brady's. In *Billy Phelan's Greatest Game,* just to rankle the McCalls who "dumped him as their candidate for Congress" when his picture appears with Diamond (*BP,* 221), Gorman becomes Francis Phelan's lawyer and he successfully defends Francis later in *Ironweed.*

Like Kennedy's other heroes, Diamond strives for meaning in his life and lives by a sharply defined code of conduct, albeit one unlike the codes of Bailey, Billy and Francis Phelan, and Daniel Quinn. Diamond's code originated in the gangster world—never inform, never reveal assassins, always retaliate in kind. Diamond also pits himself against rival mobsters, neophyte punks aspiring to greatness, politicians craving fame, and local, state, and federal police forces. The constant in Diamond's characterization remains his will to survive as he constantly renews "his vulnerability to punishment, death, and damnation" (*L,* 188), revealing a determination that suggests Bailey's always running to a clubbing, Billy Phelan's refusing to cooperate with the McCalls, Francis Phelan's battling the ghosts of his past, and Daniel Quinn's transcending life's negative forces.

According to Kennedy, one of his major themes is regeneration. Thus Legs Diamond's death becomes his regeneration in that he is reborn into myth and thus transcends the final historical image of the underwear-clad corpse. In short, he emerges from the underworld sludge to become the "dude of all gangsters" who amasses a ten-million-dollar empire, who leaves a "legacy of money and guns that would dominate the American city on through the 1970s," and who becomes "unquestionably an ancestral paradigm for modern urban political gangsters" (*L,* 215). Or, as Gorman remarks, "Not . . . bad . . . for a little street kid from Philly" (*L,* 232).

Second and succeeding novels are often better than first ones, and such is the case with *Legs,* about which Kennedy says, "I began to understand writing a little more clearly."[26] First of all, in adapting the gangster novel in *Legs,* Kennedy makes major contributions to this minor genre. Moreover, each element in *Legs*—point-of-view, narrative sequences, characterizations, setting, and balance between myth and realism—complements and highlights the others while contributing to the novel's purpose: explaining why the public was fascinated with Diamond and how he became part of America's myth. Finally, in *Legs,* the interactions of fictional characters with historical people, places, and events foreshadow *Billy Phelan's Greatest Game, Ironweed,* and *Quinn's Book.*

Chapter Five
"The Author's Creation":
Billy Phelan's Greatest Game

In reviewing William Kennedy's *Billy Phelan's Greatest Game,* Philip Corwin writes that, with the exception of Martin Daugherty, the novel contains only "repugnant characters" and Kennedy's primary concern is "invoking a feeling of time" instead of "conveying a message."[1] Jack Oakley claims that Martin Daugherty's "mind excursions into religion, philosophy, and the past" distract the reader, that Billy Phelan does not solve his dilemma, and that Billy and Daugherty lack Diamond's "vitality and charm."[2] Although admiring the novel's surface that is "polished to a high gloss" and the distracting details that are "expertly done," Peter S. Prescott concludes that "the plot seems no more to have engaged its author's interest than it did mine" and that the plot details do not "coalesce" and so the story never progresses.[3]

These early reviewers, however, have generally misread *Billy Phelan.* Not only are there other redeeming characters besides Daugherty—for example, Margaret Elizabeth Quinn, Annie Phelan, and especially Billy—but even the "repugnant" characters are recognizably human in their idiosyncrasies, foibles, and fortunes. Furthermore, the "feeling of time," which Kennedy always evokes, interconnects with and is essential for the novel's sense of place and theme. Daugherty's "mind excursions" are vital to his characterization and to the novel's secondary plot which focuses on him and his conflict, and Billy Phelan acts positively by following his own stylized code of behavior. Moreover, Daugherty and Billy are not Diamond's clones but are rather new, different characters who possess their own vitality and charm, or, as Kennedy emphasizes in the "Preface," they are the "result of the author's creation." Daugherty's originality lies in his sense of humor and accurate assessment of himself, and Billy Phelan's in his sassy boldness that certainly matches Diamond's vivacity and charm. Prescott's observation is faulty in that the parallel plots involving Daugherty and Billy merge, separate, and merge again as the novel progresses to its denouement.

On the other hand, Doris Grumbach, who lived in Albany for twenty years and who gave the opening lecture for Albany's four-day celebration honoring Kennedy, praises *Billy Phelan's Greatest Game* for its "comic spirit, conveyed by a tumult of fierce and wonderful language," its detailed sense of place (Kennedy "knows every bar, store, bowling alley, pool hall, and whore house"), and its "entire *Decameron* of anecdotes, memories, and details of small lives" that "enriches the narrative."[4] Loxley F. Nichols notes that *Billy Phelan* "marks a transition": "In *Legs* a single character acts upon and thus creates Albany, whereas in this third novel the place itself molds and ultimately identifies the character. As in *Legs* its plot is built on an excerpt of Albany's history, but here the nonfictional element provides context rather than focus and instead of one central figure there are two. Billy Phelan, a 'kid' of thirty, a gambler and a sport, single and untested, is balanced against Martin Daugherty, a fifty-year-old newspaperman, a husband and a father, a man weighted with responsibility."[5] Grumbach and Nichols have indeed pinpointed the narrative and stylistic strengths of *Billy Phelan's Greatest Game*.

In a preface to *Billy Phelan,* Kennedy asserts that Albany "exists in the real world," but "there are no authentically real people in these pages . . . Any reality attaching to any character is the result of the author's creation, or his own interpretation of history. This applies not only to Martin Daugherty and Billy Phelan, to Albany politicians, newsmen, and gamblers, but also to Franklin D. Roosevelt, Thomas E. Dewey, Henry James, Damon Runyon, William Randolph Hearst, and any number of other creatures of the American imagination." Because Kennedy translates history and concentrates on fictional characters—in *Legs* he was tied to facts about Diamond's life and times—*Billy Phelan's Greatest Game* contains a more detailed sense of Albany and its history which interconnects with and complements the novel's plot, setting, characterization, and theme.

Nighttown: The Setting and the Political Theme

In commenting about the novel's setting and political theme, Kennedy says, "Basically *Billy Phelan* is a political novel. It's all about the power of a few politicians to control everybody's life, right down to the lowly hustler on the street who only wants to play pool and cards, and they can lock him out of every bar in town just by putting the word out."[6] The "few politicians" are the McCalls: "Patsy, the savior, the *sine qua non,* becoming the party leader and patron; Matt, the lawyer, becoming the political strategist and spokesman;

and Benjamin, called Bindy, the sport, taking over as Mayor of Nighttime City,"[7] all of whom have counterparts in Albany's O'Connells.

Except for scenes at the Phelan home and the ransom scene in New York, the major action in *Billy Phelan* occurs in Albany's Nighttown, the center of which is Broadway and Billy's milieu:

Albany's river of bright white lights, the lights on in the Famous Lunch, still open, and the dark, smoky reds of Brockley's and Becker's neon tubes, and the tubes also shaping the point over the door of the American Hotel, and the window of Louie's pool room lit up, where somebody was still getting some action, and the light on in the Waldorf restaurant, where pimps worked out of and where you could get a baked apple right now if you needed one, and the lights of the Cadillac Cafeteria with pretty great custard pie, and the lights on in the upper rooms of the Cadillac Hotel, where the Greek card game was going on and where Broadway Frances was probably turning a customer upside down and inside out . . . and the lights in the stairway to the Monte Carlo, where the action would go on until everybody ran out of money or steam . . . The lights are on because it's not quite half past eleven on Broadway and some movies are still not out and plenty of people are waiting for the westbound train just now pulling into Union Station . . . Lights are on in Gleason's Grill, which was a soda fountain before beer came back, and lights are shining in the other direction, up toward Orange Street and Little Harlem, like Broadway but only a block long. (*BP,* 132–33)

In addition to its glare of gaudy lights, drinking, gambling, hustling, and whoring, sudden violence and death punctuate Nighttown. Billy Phelan, for example, threatens to throw hot coffee in Eddie Saunders' eyes unless Saunders drops his knife. A would-be holdup man is pummeled by his intended victims, and Billy Phelan and Morrie Berman severely beat a Cuban pimp and trash his apartment because he pimps for his own sister. In Nighttime City, death is often sudden and enigmatic. When Billy bowls a 299 game to beat Scotty Streck, Albany's best bowler, Streck dies of a heart attack, and its suddenness is underscored when Charlie Boy McCall exclaims, "Holy Mother of God, that was a quick decision" (*BP,* 13). Louis "Daddy Big" Dugan drowns in his own vomit after drinking too much; and when the McCalls mark him "lousy," Georgie "the Syph" Fox hurls himself off the Hawk Street viaduct, falls seventy feet, and splatters on the pavement.

As Martin Daugherty recalls Broadway's history, especially during the violent 1901 trolley strike, he emphasizes that Broadway is "then and now, full of men capable of violent deeds to achieve their ends" (*BP,* 104). Daugherty's realization not only applies to those incidents mentioned above, but it also suggests Nighttown's darker underside as revealed in Charlie Boy McCall's kidnapping by Hubert Maloy and Honey Curry, Albany's most important hoodlums, and in the career of Morrie Berman, a former drinking pal of Legs Diamond and an ex-pimp in whom the "worthy Berman family strain had gone slightly askew" (*BP,* 14).

Included in Nighttown's darker underside is the McCalls' ubiquitous and corrupt political power with its tentacles that spread through Nighttown and all of Albany County. Bindy McCall oversees and controls "all the action in Albany . . . gambling houses, horse rooms, policy, clearing house, card games, one-armed bandits, punch boards. Playing games in Albany meant that you first got the okay from Bindy or one of his lieutenants, then delivered your dues, which Bindy counted nightly in his office on Lodge Street. The tribute wasn't Bindy's alone. It sweetened the kitty for the whole McCall machine" (*BP,* 60). In recalling his own experiences, Kennedy emphasizes the O'Connells' power that would be mirrored in *Billy Phelan* by the fictional McCalls: "Even as a child I knew it was a unique situation to have this absolutely wide-open city where gambling was condoned by the powers who ran the town . . . So what we had in Albany during that period is a unique city, a unique social situation in which power came from the top right down to the gutter, which is what I wanted to show in *Billy Phelan*."[8] Because Billy Phelan's world and livelihood revolve around Nighttown, Bindy McCall sanctions Billy's job at Riley's Lake House and his right to take bets for which he pays ten dollars a week in tribute to Pop O'Rourke, the Ninth Ward's Democratic leader.

Billy Phelan's Greatest Game also details the McCalls' pervasive power. When the *Sentinel* dredges up "The Love Nest Tragedy of 1908" about Edward Daugherty's scandalous affair with Melissa Spencer, Patsy McCall rigs Daugherty's libel suit against the newspaper—"saw to it that the judge in the case was attuned to the local realities, saw to it also that a hand-picked jury gave proper consideration to Patsy's former Colonie Street neighbor" (*BP,* 47). The McCalls' power is also relentless: "*The Sentinel* publicly admitted the forgery and paid nominal libel damages. But then it found its advertisers withdrawing *en masse* and its tax assessment quintupled. Within a month the ragbag sons of bitches closed up shop and left town, and moral serenity returned to Albany as McCall Democracy won the day" (*BP,* 47). In another incident, the McCalls black out Albany, part of Colonie, Watervliet, and Cohoes when Thomas E. Dewey excoriates Albany's corrupt politicians in a radio address.

The McCalls' vengeance is most devastating to those who offend them— "The McCalls hurl thunderbolts when affronted" (*BP,* 47). When Jigger Bigley arrives drunk at a political rally and Patsy McCall chastises him,

Bigley quits his job and moves to Cleveland. The McCalls also close Broadway to those who fall from their grace (as Bob Murphy falls from O'Connell grace in *O Albany!*). When Georgie Fox, for instance, steals Daddy Big's pistol, he loses it in a flubbed post office robbery, and Daddy Big serves two years in prison. Since Daddy Big is Bindy McCall's cousin, word goes out to Broadway, and Georgie Fox is "marked lousy." After living two years "like a mole," Fox commits suicide because in essence, "Georgie was dead long before he hit the pavement, sucked dry at Bindy's order" (*BP,* 88). Georgie's fall from McCall grace and subsequent banishment foreshadow Billy Phelan's fall once he refuses to cooperate with the McCalls regarding Charlie Boy's kidnapping. Although Kennedy admits that he is "absolutely fascinated" by Albany's Democratic machine and has "an affectionate regard for many of the people in the machine," he adds, "the portrait of the Machine in *Billy Phelan* is meant to show just how powerful it was."[9]

Billy Phelan: The Major Focus

Billy Phelan's Greatest Game, like *Legs,* has two principal characters, Billy Phelan and Martin Daugherty. And just as *Legs* focuses primarily on Jack Diamond, *Billy Phelan* focuses on Billy, to whom most of the chapters are devoted. In addition, a major portion of the action occurs in Nighttown, Billy Phelan's world where he makes his own way after Francis Phelan abandons family and home when Billy is nine years old. From hanging around Ronan's clubroom, organizing crap games after Sunday Mass, and bowling at the Knights of Columbus, Billy becomes a brassy poker player, pool hustler, small-time bookie, and bon vivant who is forged and refined by his experiences in Albany's Nighttown:

Billy's native arrogance might have been a gift of miffed genes, then come to splendid definition through tests to which a street like Broadway puts a young man on the make: tests designed to refine a breed, enforce a code, exclude all simps and gumps, and deliver into the city's life a man worthy of functioning in this age of nocturnal supremacy. Men like Billy Phelan, forged in the brass of Broadway, send in the time of their splendor, telegraphic statements of mission: I, you bums, am a winner. And that message, however devoid of Christ-like, other-cheekery, dooms the faint-hearted Scottys of the night, who must sludge along, never knowing how it feels to spill over with the small change of sassiness. (*BP,* 8)

Throughout the narrative, Billy Phelan is a winner; he beats Scotty Streck in bowling; he bluffs Lemon Lewis in a cardgame; he deliberately loses the pool game with Doc Fay so he will not owe Morrie Berman fifty dollars; and he wins the game with the McCalls, Billy's greatest game.

As suggested by the novel's title and the epigraph from Huizinga that all of society's "greatest archetypal activities are permeated with play," Billy Phelan's Nighttown life revolves around games ranging from poker and pool to bowling and betting, and Billy "roamed through the grandness of all games, yeoman here, journeyman there, low-level maestro unlikely to transcend, either as a gambler, card dealer, dice or pool shooter" (*BP,* 6). Billy knows, accepts, and abides by the rules that games and life itself require. When he refuses to pay Simpson the ten dollars and Pop O'Rourke says "there are rules," Billy replies, "I play by them" (*BP,* 67). When he loses on Daugherty's three-horse parlay, Billy tells Martin on several occasions, "What do you do when you lose? You pay" (*BP,* 72). Billy emphasizes abiding by the rules when he tells George Quinn, his brother-in-law, that the McCalls expect "heavier dues" for covering larger bets: "George, you been in this racket for fifteen years, and you been in this town all your life. You know how it works . . . Don't cry the blues to them. Don't beg for anything. If they say pay, just pay and shut up about it" (*BP,* 160). In his newspaper article about the 299 bowling game, Daugherty writes that Billy is a "gamester who accepted the rules and played by them, but who also played above them" (*BP,* 200).

The novel contains, moreover, metaphorical games. Even Kennedy says that in *Billy Phelan* "just about every form of game you can imagine is being played out in that book. But that notion of play, the way people live life as a game, has always been valuable to me."[10] Angie Velez plays a sexual game with Billy by feigning pregnancy to test his feelings about her, and Melissa Spencer plays a sexual game with Martin Daugherty so she can acquire Edward Daugherty's ledger to use as leverage in fostering her film career. Martin Daugherty's dilemmas even result from his playing mind games with himself and about which he generalizes: "How simple this psychic game is, once you know the rules" (*BP,* 177). Charlie Boy McCall's kidnapping is also a game with certain rules and indeed higher and deadlier stakes. Pimping, gambling, and even life itself are all governed by certain, and often unwritten, rules that determine a character's personality and worth.

Whether in a game of skill or the game of life, Billy Phelan lives by his own stylized code of honor that is forged in Nighttown's sludge and neither tarnished by his experiences nor sullied by those with whom he associates. For example, in a card game, Billy minimizes Bump Oliver's cheating. "The cheater lost money," says the narrator and adds, "Nobody knew Bump was really a wicked fellow at heart. Nobody knew either, how Billy absolutely neutralized him. Billy, you're a goddamned patent-leather wonder" (*BP*, 123). Even after Daddy Big calls him a "bum," Billy prevents him from choking to death when Daddy Big passes out on the street. In another incident, Billy sees Georgie Fox knock down Mrs. Slyer and take four dollars out of her purse, and Billy tells Daugherty, "I wouldn't rat even on a bum like Georgie. What I did the next time I saw him was kick him in the balls before he could say anything and take twenty off him and mail it to Mrs. Slyer" (*BP*, 105–106). After Angie's sexual ploy fails, she pinpoints Billy's stylized code: "You're a life-bringer, Billy. You're the real man for me, but you're the wrong clay . . . You can't be molded. Sex won't do it and money won't. Even the idea of the kid wouldn't. But you did say you'd go along with me. That's really something" (*BP*, 168).

The novel's main conflict emphasizes the depth of Billy's code. Patsy and Bindy McCall want him to spy on Morrie Berman, Billy's friend and frequent financial backer. If Billy cooperates, the McCalls assure him, "you got one hell of a future in this town . . . For a starter we clear up your debt with Martin Daugherty. And you never worry about anything again. Your family the same" (*BP*, 155). Bindy even promises to arrange a meeting between Billy and Billy's father, Francis, whom Billy has not seen in twenty-two years. Like Bailey in *The Ink Truck,* Billy faces a dilemma that damns him either way. If he does not cooperate with the McCalls they will mark him "lousy"; if he spies on Berman, "all anybody on Broadway needed to hear was that Billy was finking on Morrie, and they'd put him in the same box with Georgie. Who'd trust him after that?" (*BP*, 156). Although he inadvertently mentioned a rumor about the kidnappers being in Newark, New Jersey, Billy finally tells Bindy, "I can't do this no more, Bin. I ain't cut out to be a squealer" (*BP*, 198). Consequently the word goes out and Broadway is closed to Billy. Although Martin Daugherty is instrumental in eventually reinstating Billy in the McCalls' grace, Daugherty must first deal with the problems plaguing his own life.

Martin Daugherty: The Secondary Focus

Kennedy emphasizes Martin Daugherty as a secondary protagonist in that Daugherty usually observes as Billy Phelan acts. In the opening scene, for instance, Daugherty keeps score as Billy bowls against Streck. Daugherty even recalls how he watched Billy as he moved into "street corner life" and there grew "stridently into young manhood" (*BP*, 7). Daugherty also watches as Billy plays cards in Nick Levine's cellar, as Billy plays in the finals of Big Daddy's pool tournament, as Billy and Morrie beat the Cuban pimp, and as

Billy converses with Bindy outside of Martha's. Even in the closing scene, Daugherty trails Billy and "Footers" O'Brien into Louie's poolroom. Yet, within the secondary plot, Daugherty confronts the forces plaguing his life. Daugherty believes that he could "even profit by injecting some sass into his acquiescent life" (*BP,* 8), a comment reminiscent of Gorman's saying his life needed some gargantuan dimensions. Daugherty admits that whereas his own life is still a "question mark," Billy's life is an "exclamation point" (*BP,* 44). In addition, Daugherty says that he is a "conundrum, a man unable to define his own commitment" to anything, and even his *Times–Union* readers classify him as a "mundane poet, a penny-whistle philosopher, a provocative half-radical man nobody had to take seriously, for he wasn't quite serious about himself" (*BP,* 25). Mary Daugherty, his wife, considers him "an aging firefly who never seemed . . . to have grown up like other men" (*BP,* 27).

The stasis in Daugherty's life results from several causes, one of which is his three-day sexual debauch ten years ago with Melissa Spencer, his father's mistress and the cause of the family scandal. Because she wants Edward Daugherty's ledger from February 1908 to April 1909, Melissa lures Martin to her Hampton Hotel room where, for promises of sexual favors, Martin arbitrarily sells his father's ledger for eight hundred dollars. After spending the night with Melissa and then giving her the ledger, Martin accepts "two and a half more days of lascivious riches from this calculating, venal, and voluptuous incarnation of his psychic downfall" (*BP,* 207). After this straying, he is filled with self-loathing and imagines himself covered in "simoniacal stink" because he sold something that was sacred to his father. Daugherty also loses his gift of foresight as a result of his sexual disloyalty.

However, ten years later when he sees Melissa in *The Flaming Corsage,* his father's last play, Martin's lust burns afresh. As he makes love to her again, he finally understands and then forgives his father's transgressions: "Seeing with my father's eyes and knowing how he was victimized by glory and self-absorption, I now forgive this man his exorbitant expectations, his indifference, his absence. Once forgiven it is a short walk to forgive myself for failing to penetrate such a passionate complexity as his. Forgiving myself, I can now begin to love myself" (*BP,* 213). More importantly, as he becomes "fatherhood incarnate," he realizes that his self-loathing results from his sexual debauchery and from his "own psychic mendacity, for trying to persuade himself he had other than venereal reasons for jingling everybody's favorite triangle" (*BP,* 214). Like Kennedy's other heroes, Daugherty must fall before he rises and gains knowledge through experience.

Daugherty's stasis also results from his fourteen-year-old son Peter's decision to study for the priesthood. Because Daugherty thought Peter would marry, have a family, and continue the family lineage, Martin bleeds "from sardonic wounds" and "rages silently at the priests who had stolen Peter away" (*BP,* 17). In a sense, *stolen* suggests *kidnapping* and thus interconnects with Charlie Boy's kidnapping. Daugherty's problem is, however, minor when compared with the McCalls' anguish: "The McCalls' loss intensified his own. But where his was merely doleful, theirs was potentially tragic" (*BP,* 22). Essentially, then, Daugherty must finally accept that Peter may become a metaphorical sacrifice to God. When he goes with Morrie Berman to ransom Charlie Boy, however, Daugherty is subconsciously plagued by a slogan, "Free the children." Eventually he applies this slogan to Peter, whom he visualizes in priestly garb "blessing the world," and concludes, "Free Peter. Let him bless anybody he wants to bless" because "when we free the children we also drown Narcissus in his pool" (*BP,* 265, 270).

In a broader sense, the father–son relationship between Martin and Peter mirrors the other father–son relationships in the plot: Billy and Francis Phelan, Martin and Edward Daugherty, Bindy and Charlie McCall, Jake and Morrie Berman. Various forces sunder each of these relationships—Francis Phelan's flight after dropping Gerald; Edward Daugherty's old age and encroaching senility; Charlie Boy's kidnapping; and Jake Berman's judgment of Morrie as a "lead slug" because of Morrie's gangster connections and life. Yet, as the novel affirms, reconciliations are possible. Francis will return to his family in *Ironweed;* Martin finally forgives his father; Charlie Boy is ransomed; and Jake hires Marcus Gorman to defend Morrie. Even Martin knows that Peter may reject the priesthood and return home. Or, as Martin Daugherty realizes when he visits his father in the nursing home: "all sons are Isaacs, all fathers are Abrahams, and that all Isaacs become Abrahams if they work at it long enough . . . We are only as possible as what happened to us yesterday. We all change as we move" (*BP,* 278).

Plot Mergings and Meanings

When the two plots merge again, the "free the children" motif extends also to Billy Phelan. Learning that Billy is a pariah on Broadway, Daugherty writes a newspaper column in which he chastises the McCalls and calls Billy the "true hero of the whole sordid business" (*BP,* 272). When Emory Jones, who fears the McCalls' wrath, refuses to print the article, Daugherty faces a dilemma that damns him either way: he can forget about the article or find another way to publish it. However, when he postulates that "Children must free themselves," he quickly adds, "True, but no" (*BP,* 272) and then sends the column to Damon Runyon. After the column appears in the *Times–*

Union, "the word went out to Broadway. Billy Phelan is all right. Don't give him any more grief" *(BP,* 275). At this point, the novel's divergent plots merge again and the meanings cohere.

Ironically, as Martin Daugherty begins to understand himself, his life, and something about the world, Billy Phelan falls from grace. Moreover, in a reversal of the Abraham–Isaac motif, Daugherty, who assumes a filial role in Billy's life (e.g., aching for him when Francis abandons the family, taking Billy to the Homeopathic Hospital to have his smashed finger stitched, watching him mature), now sacrifices himself by writing the article chastising the McCalls' treatment of Billy. At this point, the converging plot lines also highlight the novel's political theme. Billy falls from grace because he refuses to cooperate with the McCalls, and Daugherty's newspaper column results from his refusing to remain a "powerless Albany Irishman" and a "piss-ant martyr to the rapine culture, to the hypocritical handshakers, the priest suck-ups, the nigger-hating cops, the lace–curtain Grundys, and the cut-glass banker–thieves who marked the city lousy" *(BP,* 272–73). Daugherty's vision has now been heightened by his recent experiences and soul searchings, and earlier he admits, "I aspire to the condition of Billy Phelan, and will try to be done mollycoddling my personal spooks" *(BP,* 200). His new self-knowledge also solves his conflicts with his father, Peter, and Melissa.

Backwards and Forwards: Character and Structure

Martin Daugherty and Billy Phelan typify Kennedy's warrior heroes who strive for purpose and meaning in their lives and who are eventually regenerated. Daugherty's regeneration comes from within himself as he battles "personal spooks." Although Billy's regeneration may depend on a storybook deus ex machina (e.g., Daugherty's second newspaper article), Billy acts positively by remaining true to his code of honor that was forged in the sludge of Broadway. He refuses to kowtow to the McCalls and refuses to leave town as does Jigger Bigley or to commit suicide as does Georgie Fox. Instead, Billy always thrives on "pressure, sweet pressure," and the pressure is evident in his pariah status on Broadway: "Billy knew he'd lost something he didn't quite understand, but the onset of mystery thrilled him, just as it had when he threw the match to Doc. Something new going on here. A different Broadway" *(BP,* 259). Like Bailey and Jack Diamond, Billy lives on the edge—"All his life Billy had put himself into trouble just to get himself out of it" *(BP,* 241).

After his metaphorical fall, Billy Phelan, like Daugherty, gains new wisdom that contrasts with his prelapsarian knowledge when he believed Broadway was *his* and that he "knows it all and it all makes sense" (*BP*, 131). For example, when Gus Becker explains that he had to ostracize him, Billy replies, "I understand that, Gus. I really understand that now" (*BP*, 280). Billy's new wisdom is also tinged with a stronger sense of reality: "There were other things Billy had to do. Going through the shit was one of them. If Billy had died that night, he'd have died a sucker. But the sucker got wised up and he ain't anywheres near heaven yet. They are buying you drinks now . . . because the word is new, but they'll remember you're not to be trusted. You're a renegade now . . . You got the mark on you now" (*BP*, 281). Ultimately, Billy Phelan's greatest game is neither his near-perfect bowling game nor the other games he plays well, but rather it is his confrontation with life's forces because, after all, life is a game, and Billy plays by and above the rules, and *above* implies Billy's intuitive values about right and wrong. In addition, just as Daugherty embraces his father, Billy, who is guided by his intuition and code, eagerly helps Francis by bailing him out of jail, giving him money and cigarettes, and inviting him home. In *Ironweed,* Francis says, "He knows what a man needs, Billy does" (*I*, 164).

Although it too relies on flashbacks that weave in and out of history as do those in *The Ink Truck* and *Legs*, the structure of *Billy Phelan* is more concentrated since its time frame covers several days that center around Charlie Boy's kidnapping. Billy's bowling match with Scotty Streck ends at two-thirty on Thursday morning, Charlie is kidnapped about four the same morning, Billy falls from grace on Saturday evening, and Charlie is ransomed in New York City about four on Monday morning. The exact time frame for the novel's last chapter is not specific, but the action occurs shortly after Charlie Boy returns home and Daugherty's column appears in the *Times-Union*. With the exception of the ransom scene, the novel's action occurs solely in Albany.

Whereas *The Ink Truck* had one principal character and one plot line, *Legs* had two focal characters but one plot line in which Marcus Gorman is incidentally involved. In contrast, *Billy Phelan's Greatest Game* is intricately plotted with two focal characters' lives and plot lines. Within the narrative frame both the characters' lives and plot lines merge, separate, merge again, and thus reinforce the interconnections that characterize Kennedy's cycle novels. These plot mergings and separations are apparent in that five chapters focus on Daugherty and develop his plot, eight focus on Billy and develop his plot, and six chapters contain scenes in which Billy and Daugherty are present. Furthermore, the novel opens and closes with scenes in Albany's Nighttown where Billy hustles and Daugherty watches. Equally significant in terms of interconnection and the cycle–novel techniques, is that Billy's plot line foreshadows the plot of *Ironweed*. "*Billy Phelan* and *Ironweed* end on the same day," says Kennedy, "and they do that only because having created the dynamics of Billy meeting his father, the logical thing when I dealt with Francis was to see him in those post-confrontational days with Billy—to discover what it was that made him go home. Francis Phelan wouldn't go home until he knew that Annie had never condemned him or blamed him. So first comes the two things: the invitation from Billy and the knowledge about Annie."[11]

Chapter Six
"My Best Book": *Ironweed*

The problems William Kennedy had with Viking about publishing *Ironweed* and the thirteen rejections from other publishing houses are well known. Kennedy felt that it was his "best book," but, because he had such difficulty with publishers, thought "nobody was going to buy it."[1] When *Ironweed* was finally published critics recognized it as Kennedy's finest novel thus far. William H. Pritchard, for instance, claims that of Kennedy's novels, *Ironweed* is the "best, and it should bring this original and invigorating novelist to the attention of many new readers, especially since it is written in a language that is vital throughout."[2] After praising its plot and characterization, Paul Gray concludes: "*Ironweed* stands handsomely on its own, but *Legs* and *Billy Phelan's Greatest Game* are being reissued . . . to accompany its publication. Those who wish to watch a geography of the imagination take shape should read all three and then pray for more."[3] The most flattering comments are by Peter S. Prescott: "William Kennedy has written good fiction before, which has gone largely unnoticed. This novel . . . should place him among the best of our current American novelists. In its refusal to sentimentality, its freshness of language and the originality with which its author approaches scenes well worn before his arrival, *Ironweed* has a sense of permanence about it."[4]

In addition, perceptive overviews of Kennedy's life and works appeared in the *Dictionary of Literary Biography Yearbook,* Beacham's *Popular Fiction in America, Critical Survey of Long Fiction Supplement,* and *Masterplots.* Scholars and critics have analyzed *Ironweed,* and some of the seminal articles include Peter P. Clarke's "Classical Myth in William Kennedy's *Ironweed,*" an insightful essay establishing relationships between Francis Phelan and such classical heroes as Odysseus, Aeneas, Menelaus, and Agamemnon. David Black examines Kennedy's use of past and present time in *Ironweed,* I have written about the circular flight motifs and the parallels between *Ironweed* and Dante's *Purgatorio,* and Robert Gibb's 1986 dissertation analyzes Kennedy as a magical realist.

Albany and Bumdom

As do *The Ink Truck* and *Billy Phelan's Greatest Game, Ironweed* takes place solely within Albany in 1938, the year when America moved inexorably out of the Depression towards a hopeful future. This time, however, Kennedy's fictional world focuses on the world of bums, the street people, who, because of either the Depression, misfortune, or an accidental, violent act, become society's derelicts who sleep in high weeds, abandoned automobiles, foul-smelling flop houses, hobo jungles, or empty, tumbling-down buildings. They either panhandle or work just long enough to buy the cheap wine or whiskey they crave, and they attend services at the Mission of Holy Redemption, not for Reverend Chester's redemptive sermons, but for the hot meals that follow the services.

In *Ironweed,* bumdom also dramatizes sudden violence and bizarre deaths. Police roust the bums from the abandoned buildings and jail them, and civic-minded American Legionnaires raid the hobo jungles, burn the makeshift shelters, and club hapless bums. As the nemesis of bums, winter also tolls the death bell for some of them. Because she is drunk and Reverend Chester will not permit her inside, Sandra freezes to death beside the Mission of Holy Redemption, and scavenger dogs eat part of her hand and face. Ponco Pete "froze like a brick"; Poocher Felton "pissed his pants and froze tight to the sidewalk"; Ward Six froze to death with a "red icicle growin' out of his nose"; and Foxy Phil Tooker "froze all scrunched up, knees under his chin" (*I,* 77). Strawberry Bill Benson "coughed and died" and was buried in a tenement grave, and Helen Archer is dying from a stomach tumor, Rudy Newton from cancer, and Clara from consumption.

Like the world of the strikers in *The Ink Truck,* the world of the gangsters in *Legs,* and the world of Nighttown in *Billy Phelan,* the world of the homeless in *Ironweed* carries its characters to life on the edge. In comparison with the other novels' extreme situations, bumdom is perhaps the most extreme since it exists on the lowest social level where its denizens are primarily concerned with "one enduring question: How do I get through the next twenty minutes?" (*I,* 24). A bottle of cheap wine or whiskey, a hot meal, a flop in a flophouse, a warm room in a hotel suffice for some characters, and for Francis Phelan, too, but Francis must also grapple with his sense of guilt and the ghosts of his past. From this extremest of extreme situations Francis must rise or remain forever fallen, and his struggle to put meaning into his life becomes the novel's main conflict.

Francis Phelan: The Focus and the Ironweed

Kennedy says, "While I was writing *Billy Phelan,* I had already decided that . . . I wanted to give Francis his own book,"[5] and instead of developing the dual focus and characters of *Legs* and *Billy Phelan, Ironweed* focuses on Francis Phelan. From the dramatic opening sentence to its denouement, the plot traces Francis Phelan's life and his journey to redemption.

Flight from responsibility characterizes Francis's past life. During the 1901 trolley strike, he accidentally kills strikebreaker Harold Allen by fracturing his skull with a well-thrown, baseball-size rock and then flees to escape indictment. Even though he eventually returns to Albany when it is safe, he leaves his family every spring to play third base for the Washington Senators. In 1916 when he accidentally and fatally drops Gerald, his thirteen-day-old son, while changing his diaper, Francis abandons home and family for twenty-two years. During these years, Francis's life spirals downward in self-guilt until he becomes a bum because "everything was easier than coming home, even reducing yourself to the level of social maggot, streetside slug" (*I,* 160).

These years entail even more violence and death as his scarred body and hands attest. His crooked middle finger resulted from a fight with a bum who sexually assaulted Helen; the jagged scar on his little finger came from punching his fist through a liquor store window in Chinatown to steal a bottle of wine; the tip of his left thumb was bitten off by another bum in a fight. When a runt of a bum, who has stolen Francis's orange soda, whacks Francis on the leg with an ax handle and shatters the bone, Francis shoves the runt's face into some dirt and bites a plug out of his neck. After drinking too much "home-made hootch," Rowdy Dick Doolan attacks Francis with a meat cleaver and slices off two-thirds of Francis's index finger along with an eighth-inch of flesh from his nose before Francis kills Doolan by cracking his skull against a Chicago bridge abutment. At the end of the novel, Francis kills one of the hobo-jungle raiders in self-defense. The dying and the dead are so much a part of his life that Francis realizes, "Bodies in alleys, bodies in gutters, bodies anywhere . . . a physical litany of the dead" (*I,* 29). Concerning the violence and death in Francis's life, Kennedy remarks that he does not "want to write about violence as such, but sometimes it gets in the way of life. That's what happened to Francis Phelan—he commits these very violent acts almost by accident, due to the situation he finds himself in . . . It's a form of war. Francis Phelan throws a rock at somebody and happens to kill him. Later somebody tries to cut his feet off and he retaliates and kills his assailant because he's the stronger man."[6] In *Ironweed,* even Francis says, "If it draws blood or breaks heads . . . I know how it tastes" (*I,* 28).

As the novel opens, Francis has returned to Albany to vote as many times as possible to earn some easy money—he votes twenty-one times at five dollars a vote but is arrested before he can collect all of the money. Because he is obligated to pay Marcus Gorman's fifty-dollar legal fee—Francis, as does Billy, pays his debts—Francis gets a one-day job filling in graves at Saint Agnes Cemetery where he finally visits Gerald's grave for the first time. As Francis stands humbly over the grave, he is compelled "to perform his final acts of expiation," not for Gerald's accidental death, but "for abandoning the family":

You will not know, the child silently said, what these acts are until you have performed them all. And after you have performed them you will not understand that they were expiatory any more than you have understood all the other expiation that has kept you in prolonged humiliation. Then, when these final acts are complete, you will stop trying to die because of me. (*I,* 19)

Francis's expiation begins the next day, All Saints' Day, when he works for Rosskam, the junk dealer. Instead of squandering his wages on wine or whiskey, he buys a twelve-pound turkey and takes it home. As Annie, his wife, prepares the dinner and is so selflessly concerned about him, Francis gazes out the window at the backyard. With its apple tree, trimmed grass, and flower beds, the scene is so Edenic that he feels "a great compulsion to confess all his transgressions in order to be equal to the niceness he had missed out on" (*I,* 159–60), and he finally says:

"Jesus Christ, Annie, I missed everybody and everything, but I ain't worth a goddamn in the world and never was. Wait a minute. Let me finish. I can't finish. I can't even start. But there's somethin'. Somethin' to say about this. I got to get at it, get it out. I'm so goddamned sorry, and I know that don't cut nothin'. I know it's just a bunch of shitass words, excuse the expression. It's nothin' to what I did to you and the kids. I can't make it up. I knew five, six months after I left that it'd get worse and worse and no way ever to fix it, no way ever to go back . . . But listen, Annie, I never stopped lovin' you and the kids, and especially you, and that don't entitle me to nothin', and I don't want nothin' for sayin' it, but I went my whole life rememberin' things here that were like nothin' I ever saw anywhere . . . and there ain't nothin' in the world like your elbows sittin' there on the table across from me, and that apron all full of stains." (*I,* 162–63)

Although Annie, Billy, and even Peg want him to stay, Francis, still adamantly independent, leaves to spend the night in a hobo jungle that is described as "an ashpit, a graveyard, a fugitive city . . . It was a city of essential
transciency and would-be permanency, a resort for those for whom motion
was either anathema or pointless or impossible" (*I,* 208). When civic-
minded American Legionnaires raid the camp and one of them mortally
bludgeons Rudy with a baseball bat, Francis snatches the bat and kills the
raider.[7] When he seeks refuge with Helen at Palombo's Hotel, she has died
from her stomach tumor. Francis thinks again of fleeing and even boards a
Delaware and Hudson southbound freight where he meets Strawberry Bill
Benson, another ghost from his past who reminds him about Annie's attic.
Instead of fleeing as he did when he killed Harold Allen and Rowdy Dick
Doolan and when he dropped Gerald—all have been "another departure
from completion: the true and total story of his life thus far"—Francis seeks
"sanctuary under the holy Phelan eaves," and as he sits in the attic, he thinks
that he would eventually move down to Danny's room "when things got to
be absolutely right and straight" (*I,* 75, 225, 227).

Francis's flight from guilt and responsibility has been circular and downward. Like the circular flight of Jake Becker's pigeons, Francis's circular
flight takes him back to Albany where he assuages his guilty conscience and
makes peace with the ghosts of his past that include his parents, Harold
Allen, Aldo Campione, Rowdy Dick Doolan, Fiddler Quain, and especially
Gerald. Francis learns that running from responsibility takes him back to the
starting point. At the same time, however, Francis's flight spirals downward,
and as a "social maggot" and "streetside slug," he reaches a metaphorical dead
end, an idea particularly evident in the hobo jungle's description—an ashpit
and a graveyard from which motion is pointless or impossible. Had Francis
fled again after killing the raider, his flight would indeed have been pointless
and perhaps impossible, but when he seeks sanctuary under the Phelan eaves,
his flight is upward and redemptive, a movement foreshadowed when, after
confessing his transgressions to Annie, he "knew he was in the throes of flight,
not outward this time but upward" and "would soon soar to regions unimagi-
nable" (*I,* 162–63).

Although Francis may have been reduced to a "social maggot," he loses
neither his compassion for others nor his defiant humanity. He keeps his
promise to Strawberry Bill and accompanies his body to the cemetery. He
smuggles soup out of the Mission, feeds some of it to Sandra, and then tries
to bundle her from the freezing night. He begs on the street for Helen and
makes sure she has a place to sleep out of the cold winds before he wanders off
to sleep in tall weeds or an abandoned building. He takes care of simple-

minded Rudy Newton, and Francis gives his turkey sandwich to a family "with a swaddled infant" who live in a piano box in the hobo jungle.

As the tall Ironweed plant is noted for the "toughness of the stem," so is Francis toughened by his experiences with life as evidenced by his scarred face and hands. Or, as he tells Rosskam, who tries to cheat him out of some wages, "If you think I won't fight for what's mine, take a look. That hand's seen it all. I mean the worst. Dead men took their last ride on that hand" (*I,* 149). Although he thinks about suicide, especially in the winter, his resilient determination to survive persists: "But after a while you stand up, wipe the frost out of your ear, go someplace to get warm, bum a nickel for coffee, and then start walkin' toward somewhere else that ain't near no bridge" (*I,* 146). Moreover, about his life, Francis says on one occasion, "Ain't a whole lot of me left, but I ain't gone entirely. Be god-diddley-damned if I'm gonna roll over and die" (*I,* 88). His determination to live finally provides him with insight into survival:

For Francis knew now that he was at war with himself, his private factions mutually bellicose, and if he was ever to survive, it would be with the help of not any socialistic god but with a clear head and a steady eye for the truth; for the guilt he felt was not worth the dying. It served nothing except nature's insatiable craving for blood. The trick was to live, to beat the bastards, survive the mob and the fateful chaos, and show them all what a man can do to set things right, once he sets his mind to it. (*I,* 207)

B. R. Johnson and Anne Mills King argue that the ending of *Ironweed* is inconclusive, that Francis either did or did not return home.[8] When Kay Bonetti asked Kennedy about the novel's ending, Kennedy replied, "I don't want to explicate it," and when Bonetti specifically commented that, regardless of whether Francis is alive or dead, he is "under the eaves," Kennedy again emphasizes, "Well, I would rather not go on record as saying what precisely that means. I think it speaks for itself. I can't say it better than I said it there. I can't say it more clearly . . . What those last two or three pages say is what Francis Phelan's condition is when we take leave of him."[9] Yet, in an interview with Peter Quinn, Kennedy emphasizes redemption and the novel's epigraph from Dante and says that *Ironweed* is a "journey through the planes of escalation into a moment of redemption out of sin. Francis cleanses himself."[10] With Helen dead, Francis has nowhere else to go except on the bum again, but he knows he cannot run away from himself, and so prompted by Strawberry Bill's affable ghost, Francis returns home to his earthly paradise.

Structure, Symbols, and Themes

Ironweed revolves around three days in Francis Phelan's life. The three-day time span of *Ironweed* frames the plot and also augments the novel's religious allusions, symbols, and themes.

The novel opens on Halloween in 1938 when "grace is always in short supply, and the old and new dead walk abroad in the land" (*I*, 29). On this day, Francis visits Gerald's grave, receives a form of grace, and the ghosts of Francis's past do indeed walk abroad—Harold Allen, Aldo Campione, and Rowdy Dick Doolan. The second day is All Saints' Day and Daniel Quinn reminds Francis, "It's a Holy day . . . It's the day we remember the martyrs who died for the faith and nobody knows their names" (*I*, 165). On this day, Francis works for Rosskam, buys the turkey, and returns home, acts which are part of his expiation and which symbolize his moving toward a purification so he can return to his earthly paradise. The third day is All Souls' Day when, according to Catholic dogma, people remember and pray for mercy on behalf of all the departed souls. On this day, Francis carries the dying Rudy to the hospital and promises to remember Helen Archer by marking her grave with a stone—"Helen Marie Archer, a great soul"—and he also realizes that "he should pray for the safety of Helen's soul" (*I*, 223). On this day, too, Francis imagines the dead Strawberry Bill Benson whose spirit guides Francis back home. Finally, the three days also allude to Dante's *Divine Comedy* which covers Good Friday, Holy Saturday, and Easter morning. However, just as Dante's *Purgatorio* ends "the moment before the happy ending when, assured that things will turn out right, we are left with some of the joys of anticipation,"[11] so, too, does *Ironweed* end with Francis, secure under the holy Phelan eaves, anticipating future joy with his family, of moving to Danny's room when everything is "absolutely right and straight."

In contrast to his three previous novels, Kennedy heightens *Ironweed*'s time frame, plot, and characterization with religious allusions and symbolism that complement Francis's journey to redemption, a motif suggested by the novel's prefatory quotation from the *Purgatorio:* "To course o'er better waters now hoist sail little bark of my wit, leaving behind a sea so cruel."

Like Dante's ascent from Hell's pit, Francis's upward journey from the metaphorical hell of his self-guilt and bumdom is implied in the word *up* in the novel's dramatic opening sentence: "Riding up the winding road of Saint Agnes Cemetery in the back of the rattling old truck, Francis Phelan became aware that the dead, even more than the living, settled down in neighborhoods" (*I*, 1). While *up* in the cemetery, Francis visits Gerald's grave and begins his final expiatory acts. The reference to there being more dead than living emphasizes Francis's waning life—he is fifty-eight years old—and the need to set his life straight, to metaphorically "set things right."

Other religious symbolism includes the various washings that Francis undertakes to cleanse himself of his bumdom stink. While at Gerald's grave, Francis smells his own "uncancelled stink" that "lay in foul encrustation atop the private pestilence of his being," and later at the Mission of Holy Redemption he washes and rewashes "the stink of the dead off his face and hands" (*I*, 33, 35). At Jack's apartment, Francis washes the fetid odor from his "genitals and buttocks, and all their encrusted orifices, crevices, and secret folds" (*I*, 71). Then when he returns home, he submerges himself in the family bathtub in a symbolical rebaptism. As he sits in the bathtub, Francis feels "blessed," and the bathroom sink, with its "sacred faucets," "holy" drainpipe, and its "aura of sanctity," forces him to realize that "everything was blessed at some point in its existence" (*I*, 171–72). As his sweat combines with the bath water to form a "confluence of ancient and modern waters," which symbolize his past and present life and his past sins and redemption, he rises baptismal-like from the waters to stare out the window at a sudden sunburst "as if some angel of beatific lucidity were hovering outside the bathroom window" (*I*, 172). After bathing, he finally and symbolically casts off the "stink of his bumdom" when he dons his 1916 suit and shoes that restore his "resurrectible good looks," an idea further emphasized when he earlier thinks about his teeth, "A man can get new teeth, store teeth. Annie got 'em" (*I*, 172, 169).

Even before this incident, Francis realizes that he may redeem what remains of his life when he and Annie "ascend" the stairs to the attic where Francis looks at a photograph in which he and several other players toss a baseball back and forth. The camera has frozen two images of the baseball, one still in the hand, the other in flight. For Francis this picture becomes a "Trinitarian talisman (a hand, a glove, a ball) for achieving the impossible: for he had always believed it impossible for him, ravaged man, failed human, to reenter history under this roof. Yet here he was in this aerie of reconstitutable time, touching untouchable artifacts of a self that did not yet know it was ruined . . . And Francis is not yet ruined, except as an apparency in process. The ball still flies. Francis still lives to play another day. Doesn't he?" (*I*, 169).

Another structural element in *Ironweed* that is not evident in the other novels is the autumnal and wintery tone that highlights the other fictional elements. The novel opens on Halloween and closes on the second day of November, a time when autumn fades into winter. For instance, as the truck rattles up the cemetery's hills, Francis says, "A little chilly . . . but it's going to

be a nice day," and after he visits Gerald's grave, the breeze becomes "temper-
ate" and the sun rises to a "noonday pitch" (*I*, 3, 20). In the evening, when
Francis and Rudy see Sandra sprawled in the dust by the Mission, Francis
warns her, "You gonna freeze here tonight . . . Gonna be frost, freezin'
weather. Could even snow . . . I slept the last two nights in the weeds and it
was awful cold, but tonight's colder already than it was either of them nights"
(*I*, 31).

While the autumnal images suggest that Francis is well into the autumn of
his life, the winter images complement one of the novel's major themes,
death. Not only does death govern the opening scene in St. Agnes Cemetery,
but it is also apparent in the number of people who comprise Francis's "physical litany of the dead." As a memento mori each ghost reminds Francis of his
encroaching old age and mortality. Moreover, when he relates tales about
dying and death, Francis underscores life's capriciousness and brevity with
"whango bango . . . Katie bar the door. Too wet to plow" (*I*, 27). All Saints'
and All Souls' Day and his realization that the dead outnumber the living
combine to remind him that he is inching toward the final days of his life and
that he must redeem what little time remains for him and "show them what a
man can do to set things right" (*I*, 207). Moreover, not only does Francis' desire to "set things right" initially apply to making peace with Gerald whose
crooked neck prompted nine-year-old Billy to ask, "Why is Gerald crooked?"
but it also applies to Francis' thoughts about moving into Danny's room
when "things got to be absolutely right and straight" (*I*, 19, 227).

The Ironweed Women

Because *The Ink Truck, Legs, Billy Phelan's Greatest Game,* and *Quinn's
Book* depict essentially male worlds, the female characters, while significant
for the plots, had minor roles. As Kennedy says, "You either went home and
there were women waiting for you who were running the house or working or
whatever, but they didn't intersect with that world unless they were somehow
on the fringe of the show business element or, you know, ladies of the evening.
That was the kind of world that those men inhabited."[12] Although the world
of *Ironweed* is bumdom into which some women are capriciously cast, the
novel is essentially about homecomings in that both Helen and Francis return
to Albany—she to expiate her sins and die, he to reconstitute his life. In addition, *Ironweed* is a love story about two strong feminine characters, Helen
Archer and Annie Phelan, who in their own ways typify the ironweed plant's
tough stem.

When asked about Helen Archer as a strong character, Kennedy replied, "I think she's completely understood. She's the context for the entirety of her life. There's reflection on it by her and behavior as a consequence of that. You get a sense of an odyssey. You get a strong sense of personality, and I think that's probably the most complete female character I've ever dealt with."[13] Like Francis's life, Helen's life spirals downward because of whim or fate. One of the first things that plummets her into eventual bumdom is her mother's petty viciousness and greed. Before leaping to death from the Hawk Street viaduct, Brian Archer, Helen's father, wrote a one-page will leaving Helen half his moderate fortune so she could finish Vassar and pursue her musical career; the other half of his estate was to be divided between Helen's mother and brother Patrick. Mrs. Archer hides the will in a locked diary and finances Patrick's last year in law school. Upon discovering her mother's duplicity, Helen deserts her now paralyzed mother, whom she has "nursed toward the grave for ten years," and thus forces Patrick, who never knew of his mother's deceitfulness, to care for Mrs. Archer, whom he sends to a public nursing home.

Helen's downwardly spiraling life results also from Arthur's selfish lust. At nineteen and working in Arthur's piano store, Helen falls in love with Arthur who keeps her a "prisoner of love on Tuesdays and Thursdays, when he closed early, and on Friday nights, too, when he told his wife he was rehearsing with the Mendelssohn Club" (*I*, 126). When she is twenty-seven and realizes that she will neither marry Arthur nor enjoy a musical career, Arthur jilts her for a younger, tone-deaf, musically illiterate secretary. Helen then begins drifting through life, sliding "down and down until hope within her died. Hopeless Helen, that's who she was when she met Francis" (*I*, 55).

Helen also may have become a "social maggot," but, like Francis, she is defiantly assertive about her principles. When Francis asks her why she refuses to sleep at the Mission of Holy Redemption, for instance, she replies, "I don't want their charity . . . Anyway I don't like Chester. He doesn't like Catholics" (*I*, 65). She is more adamant in her Catholicism than is Francis, carries her rosary until it is stolen, and hears Mass on All Saints' Day. As does Francis, Helen accepts responsibility for her own decisions and actions. For example, she does not blame Arthur: "She knows you were a man of frail allegiance in a way that Francis never was: knows too that she allowed you to hurt her" (*I*, 134). Helen's inner strength is also evident in that she neither commits suicide like her father nor slices her wrists and bleeds "her life away in her lover's bathtub" like Edna (*I*, 56). Finally, even though she dies "at the end of the end bed in the end room of the end hotel of the end city of the end," she defiantly claims that she is certainly "no symbol of lost anything, wrong-road-taken kind of person, if they-only-knew-her-then kind of person" (*I*, 135).

Helen may have returned to Albany to die, but she expiates her sins and dies at peace with herself, the world, and God because she dies out of love. Her real ironweed strength resides in her decision to free Francis so he can return to his family—to sever her subservience to him which has "perpetuated his relationship to her for most of their nine years" (I, 121). She even suggests that he visit his family, and when she walks away from him in the early hours of All Saints' Day, she decides she will not meet him later at the Mission: "Helen was giving help of her own to Francis now by staying away from him," and during All Saints' Day Mass she offers "up a Hail Mary so he would be given divine guidance with his problems. The poor man was so guilty" (I, 121). Her selfless love for Francis becomes finally evident when she concludes:

She never betrayed anybody, and that, in the end, is what counts with her. She admits she is leaving Francis, but no one could call that betrayal. One might, perhaps, call it abdication, the way the King of England abdicated for the woman he loved. Helen is abdicating for the man she used to love so he can be as Helen wants him to be . . . Didn't Francis beg on the street for Helen when she was sick in '33? Why, he never even begged for himself before that. If Francis could become a beggar out of love, why can't Helen abdicate for the same reason?" (I, 138)

In Helen's final moments, she expiates her sins by acknowledging her failings and foibles. Her death thus becomes a transcendence as she feels blessed, an idea emphasized by Beethoven's "Ode to Joy," the record she hears in the music store, and by the gospel she hears during All Saints' Day Mass— "Blessed are ye when they shall revile you, and persecute you, and speak all that is evil against you, untruly, for my sake: be glad and rejoice, for your reward is very great in heaven" (I, 123).

If Helen is the context for her life so is Annie Phelan who, as another ironweed plant with stronger stems and roots, may represent what Helen might have become had not fate intervened. Various parallels exist between Helen and Annie. Both are staunch Catholics, both love Francis for who he is, and both lose a child fathered by Francis—Annie loses Gerald and Helen miscarries. These examples aside, in contrast to Helen's bumdom, Annie is a hearth goddess who symbolizes stability and eventually regeneration for Francis.

Just as Helen's tattered clothes represent her Quixotic bumdom, Annie's appearance highlights her hearth goddess role. Her hands are red from house work and her apron is stained from cooking. Not only does she raise Peg and Billy well—"Grew up nice, Billy did . . . Couple of tough bozos you raised, Annie," says Francis—but Annie can boast, "We can pay our way . . . We've had bad times but we can still pay the rent. And we've never gone hungry" (*I*, 180, 183). Annie has also reserved a site in the family burial plot for Francis because, as she reminds him, he is still part of the family. In her hearth goddess role, Annie also preserves the family's annals. She keeps Francis's trunk that contains artifacts from his past: newspaper clippings, old photographs, his 1916 clothes, and his baseball shoes, hat, and glove, all of which enable him to reconstitute his life and return home.

Annie's magnanimity is her most enduring hearth goddess virtue. She never tells Peg and Billy that Francis dropped Gerald, and in *Billy Phelan's Greatest Game* she explains why:

But she wouldn't hold an accident against a man as good as Francis was and who loved the children so and was only weak, for you can hate the weakness but not the man . . . I kept it from you both because I didn't want you to hate him more than you did . . . Because when a good man dies, it's reason to weep, and he died that day and we wept and he went away and buried himself and he's dead now, dead and can't be resurrected. So don't hate him and worry him, and try to understand that not everything that happens on this earth has a reason behind it that you can find in a prayer book. Not even the priests have answers for things like this. It's a mystery we can't solve any more than we can solve the meaning of the stars. Let the man be, for the love of the sweet infant Jesus, let the man be. (*BP*, 249–50)

Annie's knowledge, compassion, and magnanimity arise from her own sense of guilt since she assumes partial blame for Gerald's death: "Only this time the diaper wasn't pinned right, and that was my fault" (*BP*, 249). As relentlessly as Francis's guilt plagued him, Annie's guilt plagues her and eventually provides her with intuitive but compassionate insights into Francis's bumdom and self-guilt: "the poor man, poor man, what an awful life he's had. Think of what a life he could've had here with us and how awful it must've been for him as a tramp" (*BP*, 248). And her prayer, "let the man be," is addressed not only to Peg and Billy but also to God.

Through her own guilt and suffering, Annie transcends and eventually accepts those mysteries of life that neither priests nor people can understand, and she tells Francis, "Nothing to be gained talking about it. It was over and done with. Wasn't your fault any more than it was my fault. Wasn't anybody's fault" (*I*, 159). Perhaps it is this insight that finally enables Francis to banish his personal spooks. Because tragedy strengthens her and makes her more compassionate, when the prodigal Francis returns home after twenty-two years on the bum, Penelope-like, Annie warmly welcomed him and "opened the door wide" (*I*, 154). Through this door Francis finds his family and his earthly paradise where he is purged, reconstituted, and regenerated. In this sense, *Ironweed* is a love story in which Helen, Annie, and Francis finally understand the value of earthly and spiritual love.

Backwards and Forwards: Setting and Character

The sole setting for *Ironweed* is Albany, and the novel contains specific references that situate the plot in time, place, and history. Although interconnections exist between *Legs* and *Billy Phelan,* with *Ironweed* the interconnections finally underscore Kennedy's Albany cycle, an open-ended frame about which Kennedy says, "I can spread out and write about anything in American history and make it relevant to that particular part of the country, but also to the country at large . . . Because Albany is in a very real sense a microcosm of the whole country."[14]

The interconnections between *Legs* and *Billy Phelan* are apparent since *Billy Phelan* moves the time frame and some of the characters' lives forward from the plot of *Legs.* The *Ironweed* plot inches the time frame forward and moves the characters' lives backward and forward from *Billy Phelan* so that the interconnections illuminate both novels' plots, settings, and characterizations. For instance, in *Billy Phelan,* Billy first learns that Francis dropped Gerald and invites Francis home, and Francis learns that Annie has never told anyone about his part in Gerald's death. Later, when Billy tells Peg and his mother what he learns, Annie pours out her grief and compassion. In addition, in *Billy Phelan* Martin Daugherty tells Billy the circumstances surrounding Francis's first flight after killing Harold Allen, a flight in which Daugherty and Patsy McCall play a major role. In *Billy Phelan,* Francis's newfound knowledge and Billy's invitation become the catalysts that bring him home in *Ironweed,* and Annie's magnanimity and compassion are realized when she opens the door wide and wants him to stay. In explaining his purpose, Kennedy says:

Even when I was working on . . . *The Angels and the Sparrows,* I realized how compelling it was to write books like *The Sound and the Fury,* with the Compson saga, and *Portrait of the Artist* and *Ulysses* with Stephen, and Salinger's Glass family stories—works that carried people, not in a sequential way, through great leaps of time, maturity, and psychological information. When you see these people in a later time, having known them at an earlier age, there is this cumulative knowledge that rivets the mind; it makes you believe they did exist in the same way you believe in that uncle or grandfather who . . . was really visually there—in that old family photograph that just turned up—long after you've heard the legends. And they *are* just as

Chapter Seven
"The Moving Mosaic": *Quinn's Book*

As with Kennedy's other novels, *Quinn's Book* received unfavorable and favorable reviews. Frederic Koeppel's assessment is that "as E. L. Doctorow did in *Ragtime,* Kennedy tries to squeeze too much into *Quinn's Book* . . . The novel draws us along but eventually falls flat in a random cluster of unrelated events."[1] John Leggett faults *Quinn's Book* for the same reason and concludes: "the freight of William Kennedy's success—all the baggage of his Pulitzer, MacArthur, Hollywood and Book-of-the-Month Club tributes—made such a load in Quinn's cart that the leprechaun got off" and hid "behind the woodpile, smoking his long, green pipe and sitting this one out."[2] Walter Kirn writes that Daniel Quinn's life is so "crammed with pseudo-historical incidents" that Quinn's characterization "shrinks away altogether" as the novel hobbles "along to a banal, romantic conclusion."[3] While praising the novel for its "ferociously charming prose that seems to have altogether too much fun by itself," Peter S. Prescott likewise faults the novel for its numerous events and then concludes: "In *Quinn's Book* Kennedy forgets that legendary figures need to rise from a real world; the writer who begins with the miraculous ends with hot air. Too bad, because when Kennedy lets his adjectives and metaphors rest for a moment he can write a moving scene in which Irish immigrants who have failed in New York board a train for the west. Nothing in this book makes us doubt his ability—only, this once, his judgment."[4]

On the other hand, while faulting the novel for "its weight of history" that sacrifices "narrative drive and cohesion to the historical sidelights" and for its "ersatz 19th century idiom that often rings false," T. Coraghessan Boyle concludes, "*Quinn's Book* is a revelation. Large-minded, ardent, alive on every page with its author's passion for his place and the events that made it, it is a novel to savor."[5] The *Publishers Weekly* reviewer praises Kennedy for his "bold departure that (finally) made him famous" and then writes that "it is *Quinn's* endless, apparently effortless invention that dazzles . . . Those who demand to know 'What's the point?' or 'What's it all about?' may cavil. But it gives a new spin to the tired notion of 'a good read,' for the reader is almost as actively involved as the brilliant, chance-taking author."[6] After likewise noting that *Quinn's Book* departs from Kennedy's usual time frame and narrative mode, Paul Gray claims that the novel "successfully captures" America's "dazzling paradoxical panorama" and that "in the past, Kennedy has excelled at revealing the dignity hidden within mean, pinched lives. This time he gives his characters plenty of elbow room and lets them move forward toward folly or heroism. But the end result is the same: a novel that is both engrossing and eerily profound."[7]

According to Kennedy, the genesis for *Quinn's Book* began in 1965 when he talked with his father: "My father was endlessly full of small detail about his life, his neighborhood, working in the foundry. I thought about how important it all was to him—of the long-dead past being so vivid and wanting to communicate it to me."[8] In 1977, Kennedy worked all summer and produced a "novel's worth of notes that were all dead in the water. I couldn't make anything come to life . . . I created characters, I defined them down to their shoelaces, and I had plots . . . but nothing was happening and so I had to throw it all away. And instead of that I wrote *Ironweed* or *O Albany!* or something."[9] After resuming work on *Quinn's Book,* Kennedy told Peter Quinn that when it was finished the Albany novels would be a "quartet, a tetralogy, a double set of twins. I don't know what you call it," but, emphasizes Kennedy, *Quinn* would be about the Daughertys, Quinns, and Katrina's ancestors, and "Albany is still going to be Albany, but I'm going backward now to discover patterns that anticipate the twentieth century present. It's a preconsciousness I'm working on now."[10]

The key to understanding *Quinn's Book* is Kennedy's emphasis on patterns anticipating the twentieth century and "preconsciousness," both of which provide *Quinn* with a greater scope and depth than *The Ink Truck, Legs, Billy Phelan's Greatest Game,* and possibly even the much-acclaimed *Ironweed. Quinn's Book* not only interconnects with its literary predecessors, but it also underscores Kennedy's continual, bold experimentation in fictional style and techniques. Whereas the earlier novels depict specific characters within a specific era, *Quinn's Book* portrays what protagonist Daniel Quinn terms an "American motley" and a "moving mosaic" which move at "inch-pace progress" and not only reflect the characters' lives but also shape both Albany and the United States.

Old Albany in Time, Place, and the Mosaic

In *O Albany!*, Kennedy says that Albany is "centered squarely in the American and human continuum" (*OA*, 7). He also says that Albany is a "microcosm of America," where "everything that's happened in the country, except for the Oriental and Hispanic migration, all happened here. I mean, you had frontiers, Indian fighting, and wars with Indians, and cowboy towns, and the wild west of West Albany—it was a cattle town. So . . . the playing out of the whole Albany plan was the precursor to the formation of the Declaration of Independence."[11] *Quinn's Book* weaves in and out of past and present time to place the narrative in the human and American continuum.

Although Kennedy says numerous "bizarre things" happen in *Quinn's Book*, he adds:

But there's nothing that hasn't been vividly documented in history including the cataclysms in the beginning of the book. They're taken from history. Maybe I've amalgamated them and made them happen on top of one another in ways that history . . . or Mother Nature had not seen fit to do, but I'm not being false to possibility. They all took place—the fire, the insane crossing of the river with that iceberg, and the explosion of that iceberg, the breaking up of the ice. Those are real historical moments that I just discovered and probably embellished to a degree that makes it more dramatic. People falling into the river from the bridge, those things happened.[12]

Elsewhere Kennedy freely translates fact into the drama of fiction—in *Billy Phelan*, for example, the O'Connell kidnapping, the power blackout during Dewey's political harangue, the O'Connells' squelching of the American Labor Party. In *Quinn's Book*, Kennedy transposes Albany's "The Great Fire of August 17, 1848" (*OA*, 67) to December in the novel's opening section. In addition, *Quinn* refers to other events that shape the destiny of its characters, Albany, and the nation: the founding of Fort Orange, the 1832 and 1849 cholera epidemics, the arrival and subsequent treatment of the Famine Irish, the Underground Railroad, and the Civil War.

At one point in his rites of passage, Daniel Quinn observes that he is "being shaped by fire, flood, ice, and the less comprehensible barbarities of men and women."[13] So, too, are the other principal characters, as well as Albany and the United States. Kennedy initially symbolizes these great, often violent upheavals in the opening section's ominous cataclysms—the exploding iceberg, the swamping of Carrick's skiff, the flood, and the fire. As the plot develops so do other cataclysmic events—the battle between the Hills and Creeks, the draft riots, the Civil War, and the personal tragedies be-

falling the characters' lives. These upheavals are parts of the moving mosaic
that anticipates the twentieth century in his other novels.

As in the other novels, in *Quinn's Book* Albany generates sudden violence
and death as evident in the plight of the Famine Irish, the Society's Code of
Conduct, the Swede's suicide, Dirck Staats's kidnapping and detonguing,
and Hillegond Staats's murder—all of which mirror the deaths and violence
in the nation itself. Quinn even concludes that violence is a "norm in this bellicose world" (*QB*, 49). Yet, in keeping with the themes of regeneration and
restoration, Kennedy emphasizes that people, Albany, and the nation can
move toward becoming something specific—an idea evident in Magdalena's
resurrection, John the Brawn McGee's successes, Quinn's and Maud's enduring love for each other, and Albany's and the nation's surviving the Civil
War.

Genealogies and the Moving Mosaic

Quinn's Book teems with notable characters whose lives intersect in
Albany's history, but many of these characters also reflect the American continuum as Kennedy fleshes out both Albany's and the nation's histories in
the novel's genealogies.

The Staats's genealogy, for instance, begins with ancestors who "descended from a pre-Christian or perhaps even a primal Staatsman" but the
family records trace the "family to the sixteenth century" when Holland "was
preparing to shape the New World in the image of the Dutch coin" (*QB*, 22).
The American Staats's lineage begins when Wouter Staats arrives in Fort Orange in 1638, eventually marries, and inevitably starts a family; his children
in turn raise families until Petrus Staats marries Hillegond Roseboom, a principal character in the novel's 1849 to 1864 time frame. As part of the moving mosaic, the Staats's ancestors accomplish notable feats. Johannes, "the
firstborn-American Staats," was an Indian fighter and a successful fur trader
who "earned the wealth that began the family fortune" (*QB*, 22). Dolph
Staats, who was born in 1644, further increased the family's wealth through
"mercantility"; Jacobus Staats constructed a sawmill on Staats Fall, the waters
from which flowed past an Irish settlement that eventually became The
Colonie. Amos, Jacobus's son, was a Revolutionary War hero, and the switch
he used on his horse when bringing the news to Albany of General
Burgoyne's surrender was planted and grew into Albany's celebrated Amos
Oak on Pearl Street. Petrus "octupled" the Staats's "fortune, becoming
Albany's richest man as the century began," married Hillegond in "yet an-
other reversal of the moral order of the Staats family," fathered Dirck, and

died in 1835. In the Staats's genealogy resides the family's "inch-pace progress" toward the nineteenth and twentieth centuries.

The Toddy Ryan family mirrors the plight of the Famine Irish who were turned off their Irish farms, forced to live in ditches, and then driven to migrate to the United States. Once in the United States, however, they were shabbily and inhumanely treated and "viewed not only as carriers of the cholera plague but as a plague themselves, such is their number . . . their wretchedness so fierce and relentless that not only does the city shun them but the constabulary and the posse meet them at the docks and on the turnpikes to herd them together in encampments on the city's great western plain" (*QB*, 111). Within the novel's moving mosaic, these immigrants' plight eventually results in the battle between the Ryans and the Palmers, the New York draft riots, and in the forming of Albany's predominantly Irish neighborhoods of Gander Bay, The Colonie, and North Albany.

As part of the American mosaic, Joshua's family history highlights the Negro slaves' plight. Cinque, Joshua's father, had been captured in Sierre Leone and had led a successful shipboard revolt; however, he was betrayed by a sailor and arrived in Virginia where, instead of being executed, Cinque was sold into slavery. When he later tried to escape, he was "hanged by his feet and whipped until he bled to death through the face, leaving a legacy of revenge and unavengeable suffering for the three-year-old Joshua to discover" (*QB*, 269). Eventually, Joshua escapes to New York's Five Points neighborhood and becomes part of the underworld in which flourish Black, Irish, and Italian gangs. Joshua also begins working for John the Brawn McGee, first as a sparring partner, then as a doorman at McGee's gambling houses, and finally as the "most adept of faro dealers, nimble-fingered fleecer of rich men in John's lush parlors" (*QB*, 246). Clandestinely, Joshua becomes a proficient conductor on the Underground Railroads and shunts "more than four hundred fugitive slaves toward the North Star" (*QB*, 240) until he is killed in the New York draft riots.

Lyman Fitzgibbon's history also contributes to America's mosaic. Born in London, educated at Oxford, and a "merchant–scientist," Lyman arrives in America when he is twenty-six and marries Emily Taylor whose family fortune accrued from shipping. Lyman also becomes Petrus Staats's business partner in the "nailworks that would become an iron-works and then the largest stove-making foundry in the city" (*QB*, 106). Through shrewd investments in banks, insurance, railroads, and land, Lyman becomes one of Albany's richest men. After the battle between the Ryans and the Palmers, often called the battle of the Hills and the Creeks, Lyman chastises those combatants who work in his foundry, and agrees to support Toddy Ryan's widow and children and to pay Alfie Palmer's medical bills, thus restoring peace to the foundry so that the "making of stoves was resumed, for now and for ever, amen" (QB, 128).

Other genealogies include the nefarious Plum family who represent society's lower rungs. The first known American Plum (Kennedy often puns on the name—two children are nicknamed Peaches and Outa), Ezra appeared in 1759, became the city's official "whipper," then official hangman, and was eventually murdered by his grandson, Jeremiah. The Plums are generally a bad lot, whose history includes incest, horse stealing, and murder.

Maud Lucinda Fallon's family history begins in Ireland where her father joined the tenant farmers' rebellion. After being arrested and transported to England, he escaped to Canada. Charlotte Mary Coan Fallon, Maud's mother, eventually changed her name, became a kept woman, and sent Maud to live with Magdalena Colon, Charlotte's twin sister. Seeking a better fortune, Magdalena migrates to New York with Maud in the summer of 1849.

Each family genealogy becomes, therefore, a microhistory that, while moving the time frame and characters' lives forward, mirrors the American motley and the events that ultimately shape Albany's ethnic neighborhoods, streets, commerce and industry, and future generations. As parts of the moving American mosaic, these microhistories symbolize America's melting pot and highlight what will change the nation and its people.

Small Mosaic Stones

Although a secondary character, John the Brawn McGee figures prominently in the novel's mosaic. McGee not only typifies the Irish immigrant, but he also typifies the American self-made man. As the novel opens, John the Brawn McGee (nicknamed for his size and strength) loses his canal boat and becomes a "river rat" who transports legal or illegal cargo up, down, or across the Hudson River for a fee. When Carrick's skiff is stove in by the iceberg, John the Brawn immediately ventures out, not expressly to rescue either Magdalena Colon or Maud Fallon, but to rescue Magdalena's trunk. Quinn notes: "My master, meanwhile, lifted the corpse of La Ultima [aka Magdalena] from the skiff and plopped it down on the shore ice, far more concerned with the contents of the trunk than with the disposition of her person . . . John the Brawn under the eyes of heaven and all the bereft, was hammering at the latch of the trunk with the end of his oar: a vision of how the fear of death easily yields to the power of greed" (QB, 11). McGee's intention of seizing life's opportunities is also evident when, in a bawdy but humorous scene, he makes love to Magdalena's corpse and thereby resurrects her, when he volunteers to become her personal bodyguard during her show business career, and when he rids himself of an extra mouth to feed by putting the sleeping Quinn off the canal boat.

Moreover, John the Brawn's story becomes another American success story when he knocks down Michael Hennessey, a world boxing champion, a feat which launches McGee on a successful boxing career that culminates when he defeats the Canadian champion and Arthur "Yankee" Barker, "the pride of native Americans," who enters the ring draped in an American flag. Within the novel's larger construct, McGee's victories over the Canadian and American champions symbolize McGee's rise to social and wealthy prominence as well as the rise of the Irish—"A sad day for the Natives, and the Green rises to the top like the cream of Purgatory" (*QB*, 244). As McGee's life continues its "upward spiral," he becomes the proprietor of the Blue Heaven bar in Albany's lumber district, the bar eventually operated by Big Jim Carroll, Kennedy's great grandfather (*OA*, 194). With gangland cronies, McGee polices voting polls and ballot boxes for Manhattan's Democrats who, because of McGee's successes with "bludgeons, brickbats, and bloody knuckles," permit him to operate sixteen gambling houses, "assured that he need never fear the law as long as there were honest Democratic judges in the world" (*QB*, 245–246). This Irish–Democratic success story culminates when McGee becomes "one of the handful of millionaires" and a principal stockholder in Saratoga Springs' new race track. Quinn deifies him: "Here looking more prosperous and fit than I'd ever seen him, handsomely garbed and in starched white linen, black broadcloth, and patent leather boots, stood the redoubtable God of Water and Horses, guarding the portal like the three-headed dog of Hades" (*QB*, 259). Just as the American motley includes the old, landed gentry wealth of the Staates and Fitzgibbons, it also includes the Irish nouveau riche who through various endeavors become successful businessmen, leaders, and politicians in Albany's and America's unfolding panorama.

With plot variations, McGee's success story parallels Hillegond Roseboom Staats's story. Daughter of a tavern keeper of "bibulous repute," Hillegond marries wealthy Petrus Staats, and to quote Quinn, Hillegond's power is "very old and reeked of money and leisure and exploitation" (*QB*, 19). Hillegond also becomes another of Kennedy's hearth goddesses who is described as a "strapping woman" with "powerful arms" and "formidable bosom" and who, on the intensely cold Albany night, warmly welcomes Quinn and Maud into her mansion of many warm hearths where, after squeezing the "frigidity" out of them, she feeds and clothes them. Later,

Hillegond also welcomes the Ryans into her house on the night Toddy Ryan is killed, and Capricorn says that Hillegond also "open her house to colored folks. She feed them, help them go to freedom. She save Joshua from jail . . . Miss Hilly a sainted lady. She in heaven for sure. She be queen up there" (*QB*, 192). Just as Annie Phelan's house provides a new life for Francis, Hillegond's mansion is life-giving. After visiting his family's "tumbledown house of death," Quinn refers to Hillegond's mansion as "this grand villa of life," and after witnessing the deprivations, violence, and deaths in the Civil War, Quinn returns to the Staats mansion "where the woman known as The Great Mother had lived" (*QB*, 78, 229). Similarly, in Hillegond's manor house, Magdalena (her name means reformed prostitute) recovers from her suppurating bite-wound, the Ryans begin a new life, and Quinn and Maud rekindle their love.

Within the moving mosaic of *Quinn's Book*, Magdalena (nee Coan) Colon achieves social prominence and wealth in show business. Having wed and outlived three husbands, Magdalena flees Europe's revolutions for America, "a nation only moderately cultural and given to irrational frenzies toward beautiful dancing females" (*QB*, 168). Motivated by a desire to get on in life, Magdalena does everything and anything to secure her fame and wealth: using Hispanicized English, crossing the ice-clogged Hudson as a publicity stunt, performing her lascivious but famed Spider Dance, and finally marrying the lecherous but wealthy Obadiah Griswold, a carriage and sleigh manufacturer and equal partner with John the Brawn in Saratoga Springs' new race track. Attesting to Magdalena's fame and social position are the "great droves" of socially mixed humanity who arrive to mourn her "proximate death." Quinn, however, lauds Magdalena for her greatest accomplishments: "her ability to survive as a solitary woman in a hostile world; her love affair with death; and . . . her nurturing of the incredible Maud" (*QB*, 280).

Quinn, Maud, and the Mosaic

To particularize *Quinn's Book* and to develop the love story at the heart of the plot, Kennedy relates the lives, times, and experiences of Daniel Quinn and Maud Fallon, two orphans who mature on the various roads of life and who grow in love. Both the bildungsroman motif and the central love story are departures for Kennedy. Quinn's and Maud's experiences complement one another, and their love quest becomes another success story in the novel.

Fifteen-year-old Quinn's initial experiences with life begin when his parents and sister die during the 1849 cholera epidemic and he ventures out to work for a tyrannical canal boatmaster, appropriately named Masterson. After running away from Masterson, Quinn works for John the Brawn. Quinn's next rite of passage occurs when he rescues Maud and pledges one day to kidnap her. Quinn's desire to succeed in life, however, contributes to his most maturing experiences. Searching for a mentor, Quinn reads those books recommended by Will Canaday, the founding editor of the *Albany Chronicle,* a newspaper Quinn "loved and devoured" and in which he read about everything from "murders and thievery, rapscallions and heroes" to war, politics, and advertisements. Quinn says that Canaday, "through his newspapers and tutelage, was opening my eyes to the world in ways not accessible to the being I used to be" (*QB,* 102).

Quinn's eyes are opened even wider when, as a newspaper reporter, "a relentless shedder of history," he observes and reports those historical cataclysmic events that shape the period in which he lives: the treatment of the Famine Irish and the slaves, the Underground Railroad, the 1863 New York Draft Riots, and the Civil War. As evident in his speech at the Saratoga bazaar about the Civil War's realities, Quinn's experiences plummet him to such depths from which he can rise only through his love for Maud, "the instrument by which he would rid himself of death and war, put life once again on horseback" (*QB,* 218).

In contrast to Quinn, Maud is precocious. When she is two years old she recites the Ave Maria in Latin; when she is four, she begins a diary, filling four notebooks with poetic sentiments. Maud's structured life ends when she is sent to live with her aunt, Magdalena. Maud's initiation into this new life begins as she experiences the cataclysmic ice, flood, and fire, the Swede's suicide, and witnesses the dissolution of Amos Staats's long-buried corpse. Maud's most significant experiences occur, however, when she becomes a "sojourning spiritualist," a "daring danseuse," and when she plays Mazeppa, a role about which Quinn says that Maud "barebacked, perhaps also barebuttocked and bare busted . . . climbed those Albany platforms to scandalously glamorous international heights" (*QB,* 204). As Maud's foster mother, Magdalena teaches Maud how to survive in a hostile world, and even Quinn admits that Maud "was learning things from Magdalena that he was not learning from anybody. Women handed their wisdom to each other, but boys were supposed to discover the secrets of life by watching dogs fuck" (*QB,* 158).

As part of the novel's melodramatic trappings, the love story about Quinn and Maud suspensefully weaves its way through the narration until it is resolved in the closing pages. In the hero–meets–heroine formula various forces always separate the lovers. John the Brawn willfully puts the sleeping

Quinn ashore, and when Quinn finds Maud again in Saratoga, she mysteri-
ously disappears. Quinn haughtily spurns Maud in 1858, the Civil War in-
tervenes, and Quinn becomes a war correspondent for the *Albany Chronicle,*
Six years later Quinn and Maud are reunited, and he kidnaps her as he had
long ago promised.

In the initial stages of their love, Quinn's ideas about love and life are pat-
ently romantic, naive, and melodramatic. As he falls asleep on the canal boat
before McGee sets him ashore, Quinn fantasizes about a romantic kidnapping adventure: "I conceived of first stealing a horse and carriage, leaping to
the reins, and driving off into the cherished night of freedom, into the un-
chartable challenges of love" (*QB*, 59). His romantic illusions are dissipated
by reality, however, when he awakens and discovers John the Brawn has
stolen Maud from him. Later, when he is reunited with Maud at Saratoga,
Quinn's romanticism goes agog again as he plans to hire a carriage, stop for
tea, stroll with Maud through the first available park, lead her into a wooded
grove, throw his arms about her, "kiss her passionately with lips and tongue,"
and declare his eternal love for her "face, her form, her brain, her soul" (*QB*,
171). Reality again foils Quinn's plans when Maud tells him to shave (his
first shave and another rite of passage). But while he shaves, Maud fakes her
disappearance after which, as a wounded lover, Quinn piningly concludes,
"Well, so be it. Forget her. This part of my life is over and I will suck up to no
one. I am done with all that tattered nonsense of first love" (*QB*, 181).

Being more astute in the world's way, Maud disappears so she can help the
faltering Magdalena and also because Maud realizes that she and Quinn are
too young to marry—"But what a proper botch would they make of an ado-
lescent marriage? It was a pleasant dream, laughable" (*QB*, 171). Moreover,
for the time being, Maud is more pragmatic than Quinn. After penning "The
sadness of bumblebees and the longitude of pity exist only for lovers"—
Quinn believes this is a romantic talisman—Maud acknowledges that "this
poetic turn" contrasts with "her pragmatic self" (*QB*, 172). In the 1858 scene
in her dressing room, the clash between Quinn's romanticism and Maud's
pragmatism results in their six-year separation. Maud says that the Mazeppa
role will make her "rich in a trice," but when Quinn says that money "isn't
everything," Maud pragmatically responds, "Don't be a nincompoop,
Daniel . . . Money is everything to me. How am I to live without money?"
(*QB*, 204).

When Maud sees Quinn after the Civil War, in which she thought he had
been killed by a cannon ball, she decides that she is ready to be kidnapped.
She once told Quinn that her breasts were too small "to show anyone," especially him, but now she bares her body for him. She further intimates that she

is ready for kidnapping when she chooses to read "Lochinvar," a poem about a lover kidnapping his beloved. Quinn has realized that his rebirth, after the *death* of the Civil War, resides in Maud, and at the bazaar she looked at him and "saw a pacific smile and knew she was the cause of it, but saw, too, the trouble that lay behind it, had noted that trouble the instant she saw him in the front of the mansion. It was the war, of course, and so she would begin with Keats, telling Quinn that he was perhaps in love with easeful death" (*QB*, 220).

Appropriately enough, Quinn has matured and resolutely decides to kidnap Maud at Saratoga Springs, itself a symbol of healing waters, of new beginnings as suggested by the opening of the new race track and the rise of the American motley in the carriage procession to the track. No longer a "vacillating kidnappee" as Quinn has called her, Maud realizes that their love has not only endured but has come full circle, the latter symbolized by her pink frock which she says is "the same color as the one I was wearing when we met" (*QB*, 253). Moreover, Maud's remarks also suggest her willingness to be kidnapped—when Quinn chides her for "pulling" his "leg," she replies "perhaps later"; when he comments about her nostalgic pink dress, she replies, "Nostalgia is not my purpose"; and when he asks her what she plans for him, she coquettishly says, "Something beyond your imagination," a comment Gordon Fitzgibbon unwittingly underscores when, in a reaction to Phoebe Strong's letter in the newspaper, Fitzgibbon blurts, "This is vile" (*QB*, 253).

Theme, Structure, and the Mosaic

Like *O Albany!*, *The Ink Truck*, *Billy Phelan*, and *Ironweed*, *Quinn's Book* is about regeneration, but the theme is developed more broadly. Quinn must fall before he rises, and his fall begins when he is initiated into the cataclysms and human barbarity in the novel's first two sections. The nadir of Quinn's fall occurs, however, when he witnesses both the Civil War and the New York Draft Riots. As the novel's third section opens, Quinn returns from the Civil War's "mudholes of hell," and later assesses his life and decides that his decision to live his life "according to the word reached its apogee in the war and then descended into the bathetic dumps of faceless slaughter" (*QB*, 187, 280). Compounded by the news of Hillegond's murder, these experiences isolate him from the "American motley" and leave him "famished for significance that has not been sanctified by blood" (*QB*, 256). He also knows he must "survive Hillegond's death as he had others in the war: move past them; control the power of grief and anger to destroy that vessel" (*QB*, 191).

Quinn's rise begins when he writes Magdalena's "proximate death notice

. . . an act of faith, not reason" (*QB*, 280). Similarly, he realizes that he has been "half in love with easeful death," a point that Maud emphasizes when she recites Keats's poem and which Magdalena's "proximate death" symbolizes. At this point in his life, Quinn's salvation is in his love for Maud by which he "would rid himself of death and war" (*QB*, 218). When he kisses Maud before kidnapping her, Quinn emphasizes his impending restoration: "What flooded back to me was not just every memory, every loving response I'd had to her, but the opening also of an entire emotional landscape that I truly knew must exist somewhere but had never been able to find: the discovery of a new place in which to live. It vanished as quickly as it appeared . . . but I knew as long as I had Maud with me I could reconstitute it" (*QB*, 287).

Maud also falls before she rises, and her fall results from the ideas about social fame and fortune that Magdalena instilled in her. In one sense, by performing the Mazeppa act, Maud has "climbed those Albany platforms to scandalously glamorous international heights" and to the prospect of a financially secure marriage with Gordon Fitzgibbon. Yet, during her climb, Maud has had "six men . . . and several hundred suitors" (*QB*, 208). Although comfortable with Gordon and his wealth, Maud's life remains unfulfilled and mimics her mother's and Magdalena's lives. However, when she is reunited with Quinn, she says, "I loathe money" and even tells Gordon that money does not matter anymore to her (*QB*, 213). Maud realizes that her saving grace lies in her love for Quinn: "He would then, in due course, be hers, never again to talk of money. They would live together, or separately, it would not matter, for they would be equals in love, something they never had been since love began" (*QB*, 206). Significantly, too, the rekindling of their love occurs in Hillegond's mansion where they first kissed—"this mansion which Maud ever since had known as a place where the miracle of love rises gloriously out of death, relinquishes its scars, and moves on to the next order of fulfillment" (*QB*, 207).

As Emmett Daugherty and Quinn watch the Famine Irish being herded out of Albany and loaded on trains for the west, Daugherty says, "They're lost, most of them . . . They've left all they knew, and all they've got is what they can wear and carry. But if lost it is, then some say this is the land to be lost in, for it all comes right again here" (*QB*, 138). And so it is, for not only in the characters' lives but also on the larger canvas does regeneration occur in Albany and in the country itself. As Quinn sits on the veranda of Saratoga's United States Hotel, an appropriately symbolic name, he reads the *Tribune* account of Vicksburg's fall about which a Confederate officer says, "We have played a big game and lost." And later a character recalls President Grant's plea for a day of fast and humiliation to "rekindle the nation's attention to ending the war" (*QB*, 249, 287–88). Combined with the August 1864 time frame of the novel's last section, these details emphasize that the nation will regenerate itself and move forward into history, ideas symbolized by the parade of carriages, an "American motley" and a "moving mosaic," all moving towards the new race course:

> Along with these, in assorted buggies, phaetons, chaises, coupes, and chariots, came bankers, soldiers, politicians, Kansas farmers and Boston lawyers, litterateurs from Philadelphia and actors from Albany, reprobates with dyed locks and widows so tightly laced that breathing did not come easy, young women with tapering arms and pouting lips, full of anxiety over the adequacy of their *botteries* and *chausseries*, gouty sinners and flirtatious deacons, portly women with matching daughters who are starting their day, as usual, full of high hope that they will today meet the significant stranger with whom the hymeneal sacrifice may at last be offered up—these and five-thousand more of their uncategorizable kind all move forward at inch-pace progress into the brightest of noondays beneath the sunswept heavenly promise of life at Saratoga. (*QB*, 258)

With the emphasis on "high hope," "heavenly promise of life," and "inch-pace progress," the spectacle of this passage coincides with the characters' lives, especially Maud's and Quinn's lives that inexorably move toward some destined future at "inch-pace progress" to "the next order of fulfillment" in life's gloriously wondrous scheme in which "all comes right again." And so the confluences of *Quinn's Book* become apparent in that, despite the deaths associated with it, Hillegond's mansion becomes a house of love; in that Cinque's and Joshua's fates are necessary so that the Negro woman "with a fistful of money" can bet at Saratoga; in that the successes of John the Brawn, Magdalena, Maud, and Quinn mirror the rise of the Irish; and in that the cataclysmic events taking place in Albany reflect similar events in the United States.

The intricate structure of *Quinn's Book* is evident in its time frames and seasonal references, in the titles of its four main sections, and in the prefatory quotations for Book One and Book Two. Although *Quinn's Book* covers fifteen years—a greater time frame than in Kennedy's other novels—the plot revolves around specific seasons: the two sections of Book One take place in Albany during the winter and spring of 1849–1850, and in Saratoga during the spring of 1850; the two sections of Book Two occur in Albany during the summer and August of 1864. Although the narrative is spread over a fifteen-year span, the seasons are cyclical—winter, spring, summer, and August as an approximate autumn. As he used seasonal metaphors in *Ironweed*, Kennedy uses them again in *Quinn's Book*. Thus, Quinn's and Maud's love affair, McGee's and Magdalena's successes, the Famine Irish plight, and the Underground Railroad and slavery issue all grow through the spring and summer sections and come to fruition in the August section. Quinn and Maud are "at last ready to love" as the novel's last sentence states; John the Brawn, the God of Water and Horses, is a millionaire; Magdalena's resurrection culminates in the splendid party for her "proximate death"; the Emancipation Proclamation becomes a reality; and the Civil War is almost over. Just as Legs Diamond's death occurs as the Roaring Twenties fade into myth and just as the events in *Billy Phelan* and *Ironweed* occur as America moves out of the Depression, *Quinn's Book* closes as the Civil War wanes and America, Albany, and the characters move at "inch-pace progress" toward the "heavenly promise."

In order, the titles of the novel's four main sections are "A Cataclysm of Love," "The Dumb Cake," "A Bazaar of Enticement," and "Tambo and Paddy Go to Town." "A Cataclysm of Love" is not only about the love that will unsettle Maud's and Quinn's lives, but also about the ice, flood, and fire that unsettle Albany, and the plight of the Famine Irish and slaves that will unsettle the nation. In "The Dumb Cake," Quinn and Maud are ignorant and naive about love and life; Maud begins her career as a spiritualist who communicates with the spirit of an emaciated man; and Magdalena loses her "lust," the "electrovital force that made people pay to see her dance" and she longs "to give her body a vacation from sex" (*QB*, 157–58). In "A Bazaar of Enticement," Quinn is enticed back into life's mainstream, and Maud is enticed away from a possibly deadening marriage to Gordon Fitzgibbon. "Tambo and Paddy Go to Town" brings the plot elements full circle and to resolution. The section's title—"Tambo and Paddy Go to Town"—refers to Waldorf "Dorf" Miller's attempt to entice people back to Albany's theater by bridging "two genres: the minstrel show and the Irish frolic." (*QB*, 92). In this concluding section, the Irish, the blacks, and the rest of the American motley "go to town"—the races at Saratoga. In addition, there is indeed an Irish frolic, the dinner, drinking, and dancing at Magdalena's "proximate death" party. As part of the frolic, Maud embarrasses Phoebe Strong for the tawdry letter and humiliating skit at the race track, and Quinn finally kidnaps Maud as Obadiah licks the back of a parlor maid's knee. The plot and characters have come a long way from the opening section's cataclysms, and so have Albany and the United States. *Quinn's Book* ends affirmatively, or as Maud says about her kidnapping, "A perfect ending to a perfect day" (*QB*, 286).

Book One's epigraph from Albert Camus foreshadows that book's action: "A man's work is nothing but this slow trek to rediscover, through detours of art, those two or three great and simple images in whose presence his heart first opened." With its emphasis on "slow trek" and "detours of art," the quotation illuminates Daniel Quinn's newspaper reporting art and the rites of passage during which he realizes those simple and great images that first opened his heart: Maud, Will Canaday, John the Brawn, Magdalena, and the Staats mansion with its images of Hillegond, "The Great Mother." Despite her detours as a spiritualist and the sensual Mazeppa, Maud's life similarly moves toward Quinn, Magdalena, John the Brawn, and the Staats mansion. Corresponding treks and detours apply to Magdalena's and John the Brawn's lives.

Book Two's epigraph is from Leonardo da Vinci: "The malevolent and terrifying thing shall itself strike such terror into men that almost like madmen, while thinking to escape from it, they will rush in swift course upon its boundless forces." Generally, this quotation applies to the most catastrophic of cataclysms in *Quinn's Book,* the Civil War into which northern and southern patriots rush "like madmen." In the same light, this quotation refers to the Ryans–Palmers battle, a "social madness," and to the draft riots during which a mob rushes headlong through Five Points to "pillage and destroy all that is not us" (*QB,* 275). It also refers to Albany's proud Forty-Fourth Regiment that eagerly marches off to battle and to Quinn who, in escaping from his own heartache, rushes off to report on the Civil War.

The Mosaic as a Fictional, Retrospective Baedeker

Kennedy says that *Quinn's Book* "goes back to 1849 and beyond. There are allusions to the whole city, its history under the patroons, taking the genealogy of one Dutch family and moving it forward from the time of the colonists in through the Revolution and up to the time of pre–Civil War . . . The past is a genuine fascination to me. I've never thought of myself as an historian, and still don't although I'm becoming more and more of one in spite of myself."[14] Because *Quinn's Book* alludes to the "whole city" and because its patterns anticipate the twentieth century, it becomes, therefore, a fictional, retrospective Baedeker to *O Albany!* and to Kennedy's other novels.

In addition to the ice, flood, fire, Irish, slaves, and Civil War, Kennedy also translates facts from *O Albany!* into the fiction of *Quinn's Book.* The fictional Staats mansion, for instance, may be an amalgamation of Albany's three famous mansions, Whitehall, Schuyler, and Cherry Hill. In addition to its fifty-nine windows, twelve fireplaces, and four verandas, Whitehall had a *dood kamer* (a dead room for wakes) and Magdalena was the daughter of one of its early owners, Leonard Gansevoort (*OA,* 82). The Schuyler mansion, also called the Pastures, was built by Philip Schuyler, a "shipping and lumber magnate," and Quinn's father worked at a lumberyard, and the Lumber District would create North Albany (*OA*, 84, 88). Built in 1787 by Philip Van Rensselaer, a grandson of the third patroon, Cherry Hill was where Jesse Strang murdered John Whipple. Lyman Fitzgibbon's wealth comes in part from his stove foundry, and *O Albany!* refers to the following foundries: "Rathbone, Sard's, on Ferry Street, which employed 2,700 workers in 1885, making 220,000 stoves a year" (*OA*, 29).

As a Baedeker to Kennedy's other novels, *Quinn's Book* extends and interconnects the Albany cycle. In *The Ink Truck*, Bailey visits the Famine Irish on Albany's western plain, and when he was in the city during the cholera epidemic he was knocked on the head for telling the people that pigs caused the plague; in *Quinn's Book*, Quinn tells of a man who yells "it was pigs running loose in the city, not sin, that caused the cholera . . . They hit him with a plank and he stopped yelling" (*QB*, 63). When I asked Kennedy if this was part of the research he uncovered or if it was an attempt to establish interconnections, he replied: "Bailey is clearly the same man who gets bashed in *Quinn's Book*. This is not my attempt to establish interconnections. This is how it happened, in my head."[15] Quinn mentions Broadway's periodic flooding, a fact noted in *Billy Phelan* and *Ironweed*. In *Billy Phelan*, Jake Berman says that an Irish mob threw his grandfather "out a third-story window in New York during the Civil War" (*BP*, 113), an act that interconnects with the draft riots in *Quinn's Book*. John the Brawn McGee's rise to wealth and social and political prominence may foreshadow the rise of the McCalls in *Billy Phelan* and *Ironweed* and of the O'Connells in *O Albany!*. McGee's underworld connections with the Five Points Irish, Italian, and black gangs are the first steps toward the Roaring Twenties and Dutch Schultz, Lucky Luciano, and Jack Diamond. The lumberyards create North Albany, and Francis Phelan first kisses Annie in Kibbee's lumberyard, one of the last yards to close (*OA*, 31). Finally, *Quinn's Book* interconnects with *Billy Phelan* and *Ironweed* through family relationships—particularly the Daughertys and Quinns—and through theme—particularly the father-son theme since Quinn is an orphan and the mother-daughter theme since Maud is an orphan.

Quinn's Book is, finally, a Baedeker to its historical time frame and to those forces that shape the worlds of *The Ink Truck, Billy Phelan,* and *Ironweed*. *Quinn's Book* provides insights into boxing, betting, and horse racing. There are insights into politics and into show business; into the era's pseudosciences that include phrenology, mesmerism, and spiritualism; and insights into Albany's newspapers and their advertisements, headlines, and prose styles. In commenting about his research for *Quinn's Book,* Kennedy says: "I worked quite differently on this book . . . I knew where I was going in a certain general sense. I knew I wanted to deal with the Civil War, with journalism, with the theater, with conspiratorial secret societies. And I knew some things about them, so I . . . did specific kinds of research—the opening day at Saratoga Racetrack, for example, I went to some pains to be accurate."[16]

In his review, Frederic Koeppel sarcastically asks, "Do we have to have Maud as Mazeppa, riding her horse in flesh-colored tights, *and* the Civil War *and* the New York draft riots *and* the Underground Railroad?"[17] As a matter of fact, we do, just as we have to have the cataclysms, the family genealogies, the secret society, boxing, the Saratoga carriage procession, and a racetrack. We must also have the newspaper strike and the gypsies in *The Ink Truck;* the death of Legs Diamond, and the McCalls' rise; the kidnapping, bowling, pool, and card games in *Billy Phelan;* and the trolley strike, St. Agnes Cemetery, the Mission of Holy Redemption, and the Gilded Cage in *Ironweed.* These events, places, and people *are* Albany and Kennedy's fictional turf. Without the "inch-pace progress" of the "moving mosaic" in *Quinn's Book,* there would be no links to the past, present, and future of William Kennedy's Albany cycle novels.

Chapter Eight
An Irish Jig into the Mainstream

In advising would-be fiction writers, William Kennedy emphasizes the importance of the imagination for creating original works:

The most serious work comes from below . . . We rarely choose our subject matter indiscriminately; it chooses us; it leaps out of the subconscious, throttles our imagination, throws it to the ground and wrestles us into agreement to give it shape. When we shape it, we define ourselves as well as our characters. Once you understand this fact you tend to trust your own weirdness . . . Original work is always weird, and different from other people's. We begin in emulation but if we continue that way we are playing the hack game. We may be doing it with all good intention toward art and literature, but it will fail unless we move beyond our own threshold, and penetrate where we keep secrets from ourselves. It is this which produces the original work, and also the original voice. Keep lifting the lid on your psyche and you'll find that you are as weird as the abominable snowman. Sooner or later you may leave your footprints all over literature (*Would-Be Writer,* 6–7).

A writer is as a writer does, and Kennedy's advice about imagination and originality applies to his works, each of which, while based on literary precedents and predecessors, is innovative, imaginative, and original in its contributions to literary tradition. Kennedy has indeed left his footprints all over the mainstream of contemporary American literature.

Because he concentrates on Albany, he is in the mainstream of city novelists who begin with William Dean Howells, Theodore Dreiser, and Stephen Crane, and lead forward to James T. Farrell, John Dos Passos, Willard Motley, Nelson Algren, Saul Bellow, and John Updike. Writers from Howells to Motley generally depict the big city as a place that isolates and alienates the individual, destroys communal ties, and erodes traditional values and beliefs. In most of these works, the city is an antagonistic, static background that thwarts and defeats heroes and heroines alike—for example, Dreiser's Carrie Meeber and George Hurstwood; Crane's Maggie; Farrell's Studs Lonigan; Motley's Nick Romano, and Algren's Frankie Machine. On the other hand, contemporary writers such as Updike, Bellow, and J. D. Salinger also deal with the city's seamier underside and its changes that affect people's lives, but within the city their characters find meaning and purpose in life. For example, although Holden Caulfield rails against the New York phonies and dreams of escaping to the west, he decides to return home and finish school. Bellow's Arthur Sammler sees New York buildings marked for demolition, pickpockets on buses, and vandalized phonebooths, but he finds a saving grace as he prays over Elya Gruner's body in a hospital morgue. In Updike's fictional Brewer, Pennsylvania, Harry Angstrom experiences those momentous events and changes of the sixties, seventies, and early eighties, yet appreciates his life and even the city he once attempted to flee.

If anything, Kennedy's Albany is more akin to Updike's Brewer in that both cities are microcosms that reflect macrocosmic forces and changes and provide stability and purpose in the characters' lives. However, Kennedy's contributions to the mainstream of city–novel fiction lie in three areas that other city–novelists ignore. First, because he views Albany as a "magical place" where the past becomes visible, Kennedy's Albany is centered in the American and human continuum. Second, Kennedy's Albany is vital, vibrant, and thus constantly renews and restores itself, as do his characters. Finally, because he finds in Albany everything he needs for the life of the soul, Kennedy depicts Albany with a great deal of understanding and love, or as he says, Albany is "one of the few towns in this universe to which the adjective spiffy applies. Albany: spiffy, getting spiffier."[1]

In noting parallels between Kennedy's Albany settings and Faulkner's Yoknapatawpha County, critics and reviewers place Kennedy in another mainstream of American fiction: the interconnected stories and novels. Kennedy admits that Faulkner's "whole creation of Yoknapatawpha was the reason I began to write this series of interconnected novels. I found the way he interconnected his lives to be a very compelling way to write."[2] Moreover, in discussing literature that interconnects characters' lives, Kennedy invariably mentions Faulkner's Compsons, Salinger's Glass family, and Joyce's Stephen Dedalus. Within this literary tradition, Kennedy creates his Irish family sagas in the McCalls, Quinns, Daughertys, and Phelans. Through these confluences of Albany's sense of place and the various family sagas, Kennedy presents a cross section of Albany's societies, places, and events that further connect his cycle novels as the families' lives verge, touch, and then move toward the next time frame or the next novel.

Bob Callahan claims that the inspiration for *The Big Book of American Irish Culture* originated when he read Kennedy's passage in *Legs* about Jack Diamond as "one of the truly new American Irishmen of his day: Horatio Alger out of Finn McCool and Jesse James, shaping the dream that you could grow up in America and shoot your way to glory and riches" (*L*, 13).[3] Not only does Callahan's book trace the effects that other Irish men and women had on American culture, but his comment places Kennedy in another fictional mainstream, the Irish-American literary tradition that includes Finley Peter Dunne, James T. Farrell, F. Scott Fitzgerald, Eugene O'Neill, Edwin O'Connor, John O'Hara, and Flannery O'Connor. Kennedy says that these writers have their own fictional turfs and reflect their own particularized Irishness—O'Neill's works contain "wonderful Celtic gloom and irony"; Fitzgerald was a "Yuppie Irishman"; O'Hara "tried to bury his Irishness" and become a "WASP clubman"; Kennedy emphasizes, however, that "when talking about Irish–American writers . . . we're talking about evolution."[4] Although Kennedy is uncertain about his place in this evolution, he admits that those Irish–American writers who preceded him taught him "how to try to turn experience into literature."[5] Kennedy's main contributions to the Irish–American literary tradition are his gritty, humorous, human portrayals of Irish life and Irish characters, or to quote Kennedy: "I felt I had to bring in the cat-houses and the gambling and the violence, for if you left those out you had only a part of Albany. The idealized Irish life of the country club and the Catholic colleges was true enough, but that didn't have anything to do with what was going on down on Broadway among all those raffish Irishmen. They were tough sons-of-bitches, dirty-minded and foul-mouthed gamblers and bigots, and also wonderful, generous, funny, curiously honest and very complex people."[6]

Kennedy's heroes and heroines are another contribution to American fiction's gallery of characters. Ever since Ernest Hemingway's Nick Adams and Frederick Henry made their separate peaces with the world, the contemporary American heroes and heroines have continually redefined their values and places in an often chaotic, rapidly changing world. Kennedy's characters are driven to extreme situations by vast, nebulous forces, and from their life on the edge, they struggle to find purpose and meaning within the confines of their lives. Moreover, since flight is impossible for Kennedy's characters, Martin Daugherty, Daniel Quinn, Francis, Billy, and Annie Phelan embrace life's stabilizing elements of compassion and integrity, home and family, and love of self and of others. Kennedy's heroes and heroines typify, therefore, those contemporary American characters who struggle toward purpose and meaning in life, who, to quote Francis Phelan, "show them all what a man can do to set things right, once he sets his mind to it" (*I*, 207).

According to Jack Donahue, an Irish jig is "incredibly fast and involved" and requires "intricate leg movement and footwork."[7] The dance's Irishness and involved, intricate movements suggest Kennedy's novels with their diverse stylistic techniques. From novel to novel, plots, points-of-view, characterizations, and conflicts become more intricate and involved—Kennedy leaves his footprints all over American literature as he Irish jigs into American fiction's mainstream.

Notes and References

Chapter One

1. *0 Albany! Improbable City of Political Wizards, Fearless Ethnics, Spectacular Aristocrats, Splendid Nobodies, and Underrated Scoundrels* (New York: Viking Penguin, 1983), 3; hereafter cited in the text as *OA*.

2. "William Kennedy," in *Current Biography Yearbook,* ed. Charles Moritz (New York: H. W. Wilson, 1985), 224.

3. Larry McCaffery and Sinda Gregory, "An Interview with William Kennedy," *Fiction International* 15, no. 1 (1984): 160.

4. Peter J. Quinn, "William Kennedy: An Interview," *The Recorder: A Journal of the Irish Historical Society* 1, no. 1 (Winter 1985): 74.

5. Susan Agrest, "Tough Guy with a Golden Touch," *Hudson Valley Magazine,* July 1987, 48.

6. "Men's Libraries, Five Passionate Collectors Invite You to Browse," *Gentleman's Quarterly* 58, no. 1 (January 1988): 156.

7. "My Life in the Fast Lane," *Esquire* 105 (June 1986): 60; hereafter cited in the text as "Fast Lane."

8. *Current Biography,* 224.

9. Joseph Barbato, "*PW* Interviews William Kennedy," *Publishers Weekly* 224 (December 1983): 53.

10. Michael Robertson, "The Reporter as Novelist: The Case of William Kennedy," *Columbia Journalism Review* 24 (January–February 1986): 50.

11. Barbato, "*PW* Interviews," 53.

12. Robertson, "Reporter as Novelist," 50.

13. Ibid., 49.

14. Ibid., 50.

15. David Thomson, "Man Has Legs," *Film Comment* 21, no. 2 (March–April 1985): 57.

16. Edward C. Reilly, "An Averill Park Afternoon with William Kennedy," *South Carolina Review* 21, no. 2 (Spring 1989): 19.

17. Robertson, "Reporter as Novelist," 52.

18. Ibid.

19. Agrest, "Tough Guy," 48.

20. Shelley Fiskin, *From Fact to Fiction: Journalism and Imaginative Writing in America* (Baltimore: Johns Hopkins University Press, 1985), 207. See also John Hollowell's *Fact and Fiction: The New Journalism and the Nonfiction Novel* (University of North Carolina Press, 1977).

21. Margaret Croyden, "The Sudden Fame of William Kennedy," *New York Times Magazine,* 26 August 1984, 43.

22. *Charlie Malarkey and the Belly Button Machine* (New York: Atlantic Monthly Press, 1986). Written with Kennedy's son, Brendan.

23. Barbato, "*PW* Interviews," 53.

24. Kit Rachlis, "It's about Time: Part Two, William Kennedy, The Years that Were," *Boston Phoenix,* 31 May 1983, 3.

25. Croyden, "Sudden Fame," 59.

26. Ibid.

27. McCaffery and Gregory, "An Interview," 160.

28. *Current Biography,* 224.

29. R. Z. Sheppard, "A Winning Rebel with a Lost Cause," *Time* 124 (1 October 1984): 80.

30. Kay Bonetti, "An Interview with William Kennedy," *Missouri Review* 8, no. 2 (1985): 78.

31. Ibid.

32. Reilly, "Averill Park Afternoon," 20.

33. Thomson, "Man Has Legs," 56.

34. Ibid.

35. Croyden, "Sudden Fame," 70.

36. McCaffery and Gregory, "An Interview," 161.

37. Reilly, "Averill Park Afternoon," 17.

38. Jim Haskins, *The Cotton Club* (New York: Random House, 1977), 34, 75.

39. Thomson, "Man Has Legs," 55.

40. Ibid.

41. Reilly, "Averill Park Afternoon," 17.

42. Thomson, "Man Has Legs," 56.

43. Richard T. Jameson, "It Is, Too, Good," *Film Comment* 21, no. 2 (March–April 1985): 52.

44. Bonetti, "With William Kennedy," 85.

45. Ibid., 86.

46. Croyden, "Sudden Fame," 59.

47. Letter to Edward C. Reilly, 29 April 1988; hereafter cited in the text as Letter, 29 April 1988. Kennedy did not wish to identify the editor who lived in Georgia or the "major editor" who declined to publish *Ironweed.*

48. Kit Rachlis, "It's about Time: Part One, William Kennedy and the Week that Was," *Boston Phoenix,* 24 May 1983, 2.

49. Bonetti, "With William Kennedy," 71.

50. Sheppard, "Winning Rebel," 80.

51. Reilly, "Averill Park Afternoon," 23.

52. Peter S. Prescott and Susan Agrest, "Having the Time of His Life," *Newsweek* 103 (6 February 1984): 78.

53. Barbato, "*PW* Interviews," 52.

54. Croyden, "Sudden Fame," 59.

55. Robertson, "Reporter as Novelist," 50.

56. Agrest, "Tough Guy," 45.

57. Ibid.

58. Ibid.

59. *Letter to a Would-Be Writer: Fiction II* (Saratoga Springs, N.Y.: Empire State College, 1973), 8; hereafter cited in text as *Would-Be Writer.*

Chapter Two

1. Reilly, "Averill Park Afternoon," 13–14, Kennedy explains that the initial *O Albany!* subtitle, *An Urban Tapestry,* was not his choice but rather a "marketing decision that was fait accompli when I discovered it on the title."

2. Ibid., 12.

3. Ibid.

4. Peter Quinn, "William Kennedy's Albany," *America* 150 (17 March 1984): 190.

5. James W. Oberly, *Library Journal* 108 (December 1983): 2250.

6. Bill Ott, *Booklist* 80 (15 November 1983): 468.

7. Reilly, "Averill Park Afternoon," 13. See also Warren Weaver, "Daniel P. O'Connell Is Dead at 49: Old Time Albany Boss," *New York Times,* 1 March 1977, 34.

8. Reilly, "Averill Park Afternoon," 13. See also Weaver, "O'Connell is Dead," 34.

9. Quinn, "Kennedy's Albany," 190.

10. Christopher Lehmann-Haupt, "Books of the Times," *New York Times,* 23 December 1983, C3.

11. Reilly, "Averill Park Afternoon," 14.

12. *Letter to a Would-Be Journalist IV* (Saratoga Springs, N.Y.: Empire State College, 1973), 21.

13. James J. Kilpatrick, "Writer's Art," *Arkansas Democrat: Arkansas Magazine,* 24 April 1988, 10.

14. Letter, 29 April 1988. Kennedy says that *O Albany!* was on its way to "print in mid–1983 when Erastus Corning died and I came back from Cornell to attend the funeral and wrote the second chapter on him, 'The Last Word,' in about two days—on deadline." See also M. A. Farber, "Erastus Corning 2d, Albany Mayor since '42 Dies," *New York Times,* 29 May 1983, I, 32; and Michael Oreskes, "Erastus Corning and His Era Are Laid to Rest in Albany," *New York Times,* 2 June 1983, I, 1, B2.

15. Thomas Fleming, "A City and Its Machine," *New York Times Book Review,* 1 January 1984, VII, 12.

16. Reilly, "An Averill Park Afternoon," 14. See also Jane Gross, "Within

Sight of the Capitol's Spires, Another Albany and Another World," *New York Times,* 13 May 1986, II, 4. An article about Arbor Hill's restoration.

   17. Letter, 29 April 1988. Kennedy says that the Kenmore's facade "has been saved including the marquee, and so North Pearl Street continues to look more or less the way it did in the Rain-bo Room's heydey, but the hotel has now become an office building." See also Shawn G. Kennedy, "Albany Enjoying a Commercial Revival," *New York Times,* 1 December 1985, VIII, 1, 14. An article with pictures of the Kenmore's restoration.

Chapter Three

   1. E. A. Dooley, *Best Sellers,* 29 (15 October 1969): 263.
   2. Stanley Reynolds, "Cosy Souls," *New Statesman* 80 (14 August 1970): 185.
   3. Dorothy Curley, *Library Journal* 95 (1 February 1970): 513.
   4. Shane Stevens, *Book World,* 5 October 1969, 16.
   5. Anne Tyler, "Albany Warm Up," *New Republic* 191 (15 October 1984): 39.
   6. Loxley F. Nichols, "William Kennedy Comes of Age," *National Review* 37 (9 August 1985): 46.
   7. Joel Conarroe, "Columnist Bites Newspaper," *New York Times Book Review,* 30 September 1984, 11.
   8. McCaffery and Gregory, "An Interview," 175.
   9. Peter S. Prescott, "American Fiction in the '60s: A List and Some Random Thoughts," *Look* 33 (30 December 1969): 10.
   10. James E. Miller, *Quests Surd and Absurd* (University of Chicago Press, 1967), 17.
   11. Will Herberg, "What Keeps Modern Man from Religion," *Intercollegiate Review* 6 (Winter 1969–70): 5–11.
   12. Reynolds, "Cosy Souls," 185.
   13. Reilly, "Averill Park Afternoon," 22.
   14. *The Ink Truck* (New York: Viking Press, 1984), 15; hereafter cited in the text as *IT.*
   15. Irene Stokvis, "First Novelists: Twenty-Five New Writers—Fall, 1969, Discuss Their First Published Novels," *Library Journal* 94 (1 October 1969): 3475.
   16. McCaffery and Gregory, "An Interview," 166–67.
   17. Ibid., 176.
   18. Agrest, "Tough Guy," 45.
   19. W. T. Lhamon, Jr., "Notable Current Fiction," *New Republic* 172 (24 May 1975): 24.
   20. Bonetti, "With William Kennedy," 73.
   21. McCaffery and Gregory, "An Interview," 173.
   22. Tyler, "Albany Warm Up," 40.
   23. Sheppard, "Winning Rebel," 79.

24. Conarroe, "Columnist Bites Newspaper," 11.

25. *Ironweed* (New York: Viking Press, 1984), 151; hereafter cited in the text as *I*.

26. McCaffery and Gregory, "An Interview," 176.

27. Ibid., 177.

Chapter Four

1. Bruce Allen, *Library Journal* 100 (1 May 1975): 878.

2. L. J. Davis, "Diamond in the Rough," *Washington Post Book World*, 18 May 1975, 3.

3. Peter S. Prescott, "Buzzers and Mutchers," *Newsweek* 83 (23 June 1975): 87.

4. Nichols, "Comes of Age," 47.

5. Dean Flower, "Fiction Chronicle," *Hudson Review* 36 (Summer 1983): 375.

6. Anne Mills King, "William Kennedy," in *Critical Survey of Long Fiction Supplement*, ed. Frank N. Magill (Englewood Cliffs, N.J.: Salem Press, 1987), 196.

7. Thomson, "Man Has Legs," 57.

8. Robertson, "Reporter as Novelist," 50.

9. *Current Biography Yearbook*, 225.

10. Quinn, "William Kennedy Interview," 70.

11. Croyden, "Sudden Fame," 57, 59. See also *Legs* (New York: Penguin, 1983), 13; hereafter cited in text as *L*.

12. Robertson, "Reporter as Novelist," 50.

13. Croyden, "Sudden Fame," 59.

14. Agrest, "Tough Guy," 48.

15. George Grella, "The Gangster Novel: The Urban Pastoral," in *Tough Guy Writers of the Thirties*, ed. David Madden, (Carbondale, Ill.: Southern Illinois University Press, 1968), 191.

16. Ibid., 192–93.

17. McCaffery and Gregory, "An Interview," 171.

18. Bonetti, "With William Kennedy," See also Quinn, "William Kennedy Interview," 68; *and* McCaffery and Gregory, "An Interview," 169–71.

19. McCaffery and Gregory, "An Interview," 172.

20. Ibid.

21. Bonetti, "With William Kennedy," 73.

22. McCaffery and Gregory, "An Interview," 167.

23. Meyer Berger, "Legs Diamond Slain in Sleep at Albany by Two Assassins," *New York Times*, 19 December 1931, 1. See also "Diamond's Widow Murdered in Home," *New York Times*, 1 July 1933, 1, 8; *and* "Police at Odds in Diamond Death," *New York Times*, 2 July 1933, 8. These latter two notations are about Alice Diamond's mysterious murder.

24. McCaffery and Gregory, "An Interview," 167.

25. Quinn, "William Kennedy Interview," 170.
26. Bonetti, "With William Kennedy," 79–80.

Chapter Five

1. Phillip Corwin, "In Brief," *Commonweal* 105 (13 October 1978): 670–71.
2. Jack Oakley, *Library Journal* 103 (1 June 1978): 1196.
3. Peter S. Prescott, "Nightcrawlers," *Newsweek* 91 (8 May 1978): 100.
4. Doris Grumbach, "Fine Print," *Saturday Review* 5 (29 April 1978): 40. *See also* Harold Farber, "Albany Honoring a Native Literary Son for Four Days," *New York Times,* 6 September 1984, C15.
5. Nichols, "Comes of Age," 47.
6. Bonetti, "With William Kennedy," 75.
7. *Billy Phelan's Greatest Game* (New York: Viking Press, 1984), 29–30; hereafter cited in the text as *BP.*
8. McCaffery and Gregory, "An Interview," 163.
9. Robertson, "Reporter as Novelist," 52.
10. McCaffery and Gregory, "An Interview," 179.
11. Quinn, "William Kennedy Interview," 74.

Chapter Six

1. Barbato, "*PW* Interviews," 52.
2. William H. Pritchard, "The Spirits of Albany," *The New Republic* 188 (14 February 1983): 37.
3. Paul Gray, "Imaginative Necessities," *Time* 121 (24 January 1983): 82.
4. Peter S. Prescott, "Albany's Mean Streets," *Newsweek* 101 (31 January 1983): 72.
5. Reilly, "An Averill Park Afternoon," 21.
6. McCaffery and Gregory, "An Interview," 168.
7. Some loose parallels exist between this incident and Jim Casy's death in *The Grapes of Wrath.* When a civic-minded raider fatally clubs Casy in a migrant camp, Tom Joad snatches the ax handle and kills the attacker. With innovations, the relationship between Francis and Rudy recalls the George–Lennie relationship in *Of Mice and Men.*
8. B. R. Johnson, "William Kennedy," in *Beacham's Guide to Popular Fiction in America,* ed. Walton Beacham, (Washington, D.C.: Beacham Publishing, 1986), 722. See also King, "William Kennedy," 199.
9. Bonetti, "With William Kennedy," 83.
10. Quinn, "William Kennedy Interview," 74.
11. Thomas Bergin, *Dante* (Boston: Houghton Mifflin, 1965), 230.
12. Reilly, "Averill Park Afternoon," 20.
13. Ibid.

14. Geneva Collins, "Novel Blends Styles: Author Idolizes William Faulkner," *The Jonesboro* (Ark.) *Sun,* 24 July 1988, 3C.

15. McCaffery and Gregory, "An Interview," 172–173.

16. Thomas O'Connor, "Hector Babenco Harvests *Ironweed*," *New York Times,* 13 December 1987, II, 31, 41.

17. "Re-creating *Ironweed*," *American Film* 13, no. 4 (January–February, 1988): 24, hereafter cited in text as "Re-creating."

18. Richard Corliss, "Slumming in the Lower Shallows," *Time* 130 (21 December 1987): 74.

19. Pauline Kael, *The New Yorker* 63 (11 January 1988): 78.

20. Richard A. Blake, "Acting Up," *America* 158 (12 March 1988): 273.

21. Peter Travers, "People: Picks and Pans," *People* 29 (11 January 1988): 12.

22. Reilly, "Averill Park Afternoon," 18.

23. Lauren Tarshis, "Afterword" in Claudio Edinger's *The Making of "Ironweed"* (New York: Viking Penguin, 1988).

24. Robert Denerstein, "*Ironweed* Director Eases Up," *Arkansas Democrat,* 6 March 1988, 7E.

Chapter Seven

1. Frederic Koeppel, "Magical Quest Stalls in Quagmire," *The Commercial Appeal,* 29 May 1988, J4.

2. John Leggett, "The Orphan's Progress," *Book World* 18 (8 May 1988): 5.

3. Walter Kirn, "Kennedy Stumbles," *Connoisseur* (July 1988): 3.

4. Peter S. Prescott, "The Romance of Olde Albany," *Newsweek* 111 (9 May 1988): 72.

5. T. Coraghessan Boyle, "Into the Heart of Old Albany," *New York Times Book Review,* 22 May 1988, VII, 32.

6. *Publishers Weekly* 232 (14 March 1988); 71.

7. Paul Gray, "An Eyewitness to Paradox," *Time* 131 (16 May 1988): 94–95.

8. Kim Heron, "The Responsibility of Carrying the Dead," *New York Times Book Review,* 22 May 1988, VII 32

9. Bonetti, "With William Kennedy," 83.

10. Quinn, "William Kennedy Interview," 70.

11. Reilly, "Averill Park Afternoon," 14–15.

12. Ibid., 16.

13. *Quinn's Book* (New York: Viking, 1988), 61; hereafter cited in the text as *QB.*

14. Reilly, "Averill Park Afternoon," 22.

15. Letter to Edward C. Reilly, 12 August 1988.

16. Collins, "Novel Blends Style," 3C. Even the novel's last section takes place in August, the beginning of Saratoga Springs' racing season.

17. Koeppel, "Quest Stalls," 54.

Chapter Eight

1. "Introduction" in *Albany Tricentennial Guidebook: Albany Still Making History, 1686–1986* (Albany, N.Y.: Albany Tricentennial Commision, 1985), 7.

2. Collins, "Novel Blends Style," 3C.

3. Bob Callahan, *The Big Book of American Irish Culture* (New York: Viking Press, 1987), 8.

4. Quinn, "William Kennedy Interview," 72.

5. Ibid., 73.

6. Ibid., 72.

7. Callahan, *The Big Book,* 15.

Selected Bibliography

PRIMARY SOURCES

Novels

Billy Phelan's Greatest Game. New York: Viking Press, 1978. New York: Penguin Books, 1983, 1984.

The Ink Truck. New York: Dial Press, 1969. London: McDonald & Co., 1970. New York: Viking Press, 1984.

Ironweed. New York: Viking Press, 1983. New York: Penguin Books, 1984.

Legs. New York: Coward, McCann & Geoghegan, 1975. New York: Warner Books, 1976. London: Jonathan Cape, 1977. London: Penguin Books, 1978, 1984. New York: Penguin Books, 1983.

Legs, Billy Phelan's Greatest Game, Ironweed. New York: Viking Penguin, 1988. Book of the Month Club selection.

Quinn's Book. New York: Viking Penguin, 1988. Book of the Month Club Selection.

Nonfiction

O Albany! Improbable City of Political Wizards, Fearless Ethnics, Spectacular Aristocrats, Splendid Nobodies and Underrated Scoundrels. Albany, N.Y.: Washington Park Press, 1983. New York: Viking Press, 1983.

Children's Book

Charlie Malarkey and the Belly Button Machine. New York: Atlantic Monthly Press, 1986. London: Jonathan Cape, 1987. Coauthored with son, Brendan Kennedy.

Short Stories

"The Secrets of Creative Love." *Harper's* 267 (July 1983): 54–58. A story about Daniel Quinn and Maud but entirely different in setting and theme from *Quinn's Book:* the endings of the story and the novel are, however, somewhat similar.

"A Cataclysm of Love." *Esquire* 106 (November 1986): 241–53. The opening section of *Quinn's Book.*

"Jack's Alive." In *The Big Book of American Irish Culture,* edited by Bob Callahan,

118   WILLIAM KENNEDY

218–22. New York: Viking Penguin, 1987. Contains the opening section of
   Legs.
"The Hills and the Creeks (Albany, 1850)." *Harper's* 276 (March 1988): 55–62.
   With plot variations, this story becomes the battle between the Ryans and the
   Palmers in *Quinn's Book.*

Screenplays

The Cotton Club. New York: St. Martin's Press, 1986. Coauthored with Francis Ford
   Coppola.
Ironweed. For Taft-Barish Productions, 1987.

Articles and Essays

"Albany Sampler: A Place to Smudge Your Soul." *New York Times,* 17 September
   1983, 24. Excerpts from *O Albany!*
"A Sense of Community: Diversity and Change, An Essay by William Kennedy,
   Complete with Bibliography and Appendices." Albany, N.Y.: State Education
   Department, 1980. 1–19. Kennedy's essay provides "a brief philosophical, lit-
   erary, and historical introduction to the theme"—the community.
"Be Reasonable—Unless You're a Writer." *New York Times Book Review,* 25 January
   1987, 3. Kennedy's perceptive views about literature and the role of the imagi-
   nation in creating literature.
"How Winning the Pulitzer Has Changed One Writer's Life." *Life* 8 (January
   1985): 156, 158. Kennedy's candid insights into his tour of Ireland, and
   Barcelona, and his meeting Ingmar Bergman.
"If Saul Bellow Doesn't Have a True Word to Say, He Keeps His Mouth Shut."
   Esquire 92 (February 1982): 48–50, 52, 54. Kennedy interviews Bellow who
   talks about his works and literary philosophies.
"Introduction." *Albany Tricentennial Guidebook: Albany Still Making History,
   1686–1986.* Albany, N.Y.: Albany Tricentennial Commission, 1985. 5–7.
   Kennedy summarizes Albany's history and continual restoration.
"Jack and the Oyster." *Esquire* 103 (June 1986): 37–40. In the journalistic style of *O
   Albany!,* Kennedy writes about ace oyster-shucker, Jack Rosenstein.
Letter to a Would-Be Journalist, IV. Saratoga Springs, N.Y.: Empire State College,
   1973. Kennedy's interesting and insightful module for journalism students.
Letter to a Would-Be Writer—Fiction, II. Saratoga Springs, N.Y.: Empire State Col-
   lege, 1973. Kennedy's interesting and insightful module for creative writing
   students.
"My Life in the Fast Lane." *Esquire* 105 (June 1986): 59–60. Interesting biographical information about Kennedy, his father, Uncle Pete McDonald, and
   bowling.
"Re-creating *Ironweed.*" *American Film* 13, no. 4 (January–February 1988): 18–25.

Kennedy provides insights into translating *Ironweed* onto the screen. This essay also appears as the "Introduction" to *The Making of* Ironweed.
"What's the Matter with Papa? I Saw Him Drink Water." Introduction to George McManus, *Jiggs Is Back*. Berkeley, Cal.: Celtic Book Company, 1988. 7–8. Kennedy reminisces about "Jiggs" and the comic strips he read when growing up.
"William Kennedy's Cotton Club Stomp." *Vanity Fair* 47 (November 1984): 42–48, 116–188. Contains vintage pictures of The Cotton Club's performers and Kennedy's comments about coauthoring the screenplay.

Book Reviews

The Assassins by Elia Kazan. *Saturday Review* 55 (1 April 1972): 75–76.
"The Last Ole." A Review of Ernest Hemingway's *The Dangerous Summer*. *New York Times Book Review*, 9 June 1985, 1, 32–33, 35.

On Cassette

"Jason Robards Reads *Ironweed*." Albuquerque, N.M.: Newman Communications, Corp., 1986.
"Kennedy, William—Reads *The Ink Truck, Legs, Billy Phelan's Greatest Game*, and *Ironweed* (Excerpts)." Columbia, Mo.: American Prose Library, Inc., Box 842.

On Videocassette

Ironweed. Stamford, Conn: Vestron, 1988.
"William Kennedy with Noah Richler." Northbrook, Ill: The Roland Collection, 3120 Pawtucket RI. VHS, 50 minutes.

SECONDARY SOURCES

Interviews

Allen, Douglas R., and Mona Simpson. "The Art of Fiction CXI: William Kennedy." *Paris Review,* no. 112 (Winter 1989): 34–116.
Barbato, Joseph. "*PW* Interviews William Kennedy." *Publishers Weekly* 224 (9 December 1983): 52–53.
Bonetti, Kay. "William Kennedy: An Interview." *The Missouri Review* 8, no. 2 (1985): 71–86. This interview is also on a cassette produced by The American Audio Prose Library, Inc., Box 842, Columbia, Mo, 65205.
McCaffery, Larry and Sinda Gregory. "An Interview with William Kennedy." *Fiction International* 15, no. 1 (1984): 158–79. This interview also appears in

McCaffery and Gregory's *Alive and Writing: Interviews with American Authors of the 1980s*. Chicago: University of Illinois Press, 1987.

Quinn, Peter J. "William Kennedy: An Interview." *The Recorder: A Journal of the American Irish Historical Society* 1, no. 1 (Winter 1985): 65–81.

Reilly, Edward C. "An Averill Park Afternoon with William Kennedy." *The South Carolina Review* 21, no. 2 (Spring 1989): 11–24.

Stokvis, Irene. "First Novelists: Twenty-Five New Writers—Fall 1969, Discuss Their First Published Novels." *Library Journal* 94 (1 October 1969): 2475. Kennedy comments on *The Ink Truck*.

Thomson, David. "The Man Has Legs: William Kennedy Interviewed." *Film Comment* 21, no. 2 (March–April 1985): 54–59.

Critical Articles, Books, Essays

Agrest, Susan. "Tough Guy with a Golden Touch." *Hudson Valley Magazine* (July 1987): 42–49, 72. Contains insightful comments about Kennedy's life and works.

Berger, Meyer. " 'Legs' Diamond Slain in Sleep at Albany by Two Assassins." *New York Times*, 19 December 1931, 1, 2. Diamond's death recorded in Berger's journalistic style.

Black, David. "The Fusion of Past and Present in William Kennedy's *Ironweed*." *Critique* 7, no. 3 (Spring 1986): 177–84. The Greek concept of time in Francis Phelan's and Helen Archer's minds and lives complements the novel's conflicts—a seminal article.

Busby, Mark. "William Kennedy." In *Dictionary of Literary Biography: Yearbook, 1985*, edited by Jean W. Ross, Detroit: Gale Research Company, 1985. 387–94. Biographical details and perceptive insights into Kennedy's novels and *O Albany!*.

Callahan, Bob, ed. *The Big Book of American Irish Culture*. New York: Viking, 1988. Informative pictorial history of noted Irish and their contribution to American culture.

Chira, Susan. "Rogues of the Past Haunt an Author's Albany." *New York Times*, 17 September 1983, 23, 24. Contains pictures of Albany and notable Kennedy quotes.

Clarke, Peter P. "Classical Myth in William Kennedy's *Ironweed*." *Critique* 7, no. 3 (Spring 1986): 167–76. Analogies between Francis Phelan and classical heroes—Odysseus, Agamemnon, Menelaus, Adonis, Orestes; interesting and thought-provoking.

"Clean-Up Diamond Gang Ordered by Governor; Wounded Leader is Dying." *New York Times*, 28 April 1931, 1–2. Background information for *Legs* and Diamond essay in *O Albany!*.

Collins, Geneva. "Novel Blends Styles." *Jonesboro* (Ark.) *Sun*, 24 July 1988, 3C. About *Quinn's Book* and comments by Kennedy about his Albany cycle novels and his admiration for Faulkner.

Croyden, Margaret. "The Sudden Fame of William Kennedy." *New York Times Magazine*, 26 August 1984, VI. A must-read source for biographical and general background.

Denerstein, Robert. "*Ironweed* Director Eases Up." *Arkansas Democrat*, 6 March 1988, 7E. Hector Babenco's comments about the film *Ironweed*, why he wanted to direct it, and film critics whom he lambasts.

"Diamond's Widow Murdered in Home." *New York Times*, 1 July 1933, 1, 8. Alice Diamond's mysterious murder adds to Legs Diamond's mystique.

Edinger, Claudio. *The Making of Ironweed*. New York: Penguin Books, 1988. Contains excellent pictorial shots of the movie's stars and scenes.

Farber, Harold. "Albany Honoring Native Literary Son for Four Days." *New York Times*, 6 September 1984, C15. About Albany's William Kennedy celebration.

Farber, M. A. "Erastus Corning 2d, Albany Mayor Since '42 Dies." *New York Times*, 29 May 1984, 32. Background information complementing the Corning essay in *O Albany!*.

Fleming, Thomas. "A City and Its Machine." *New York Times Book Review*, 1 January 1984, 11–12. Interesting comments and perspectives for *O Albany!*.

Gibb, Robert. "The Life of the Soul: William Kennedy, Magical Realist." Diss., Lehigh University, 1986. Seminal ideas regarding Kennedy and magical realism.

Greeley, Andrew. "*Agon* and *Empathos*: A Challenge to Popular Culture." *Popular Culture Association Newsletter* 15, no. 2 (April 1988): 2–5. Uses scene from *Ironweed* film to argue *empathos* for critics' reactions to film and literature.

Haskins, Jim. *The Cotton Club*. New York: Random House, 1977. Provides important historical and pictorial background for the film, *The Cotton Club*.

Heron, Kim. "The Responsibility of Carrying the Dead." *New York Times Book Review*, 22 May 1988, 4. Kennedy comments about *Quinn's Book*, Albany, and his cycle novels.

Jameson, Richard. "It Is, Too, Good." *Film Comment* 21, no. 2 (March–April 1985): 51–53. Reviews and defends *The Cotton Club* film.

Johnson, B. R. "William Kennedy." In *Beacham's Popular Fiction in America*, edited by Walton Beacham. Washington D.C.: Beacham Publishing Company, 1986. General overview of Kennedy's literary significance, biographical details, and analysis of *Ironweed*.

King, Anne Mills. "William Kennedy." In *Critical Survey of Long Fiction Supplement*, edited by Frank N. Magill. Englewood Cliffs, N.J.: Salem Press, 1987. Interesting analysis of *The Ink Truck*, *Legs*, *Billy Phelan*, and *Ironweed*.

McCaffery, Larry and Sinda Gregory. *Alive and Writing: Interviews with American Authors of the 1980s*. Chicago: University of Illinois Press, 1987. Establishes literary perspectives with interviews of thirteen authors, including Kennedy.

McNamee, Dardis. "The Making of *Ironweed*." *Capitol Region Magazine* 3, no. 12 (December 1987). About the film, its filming, settings, stars, and extras.

"Men's Libraries: Five Passionate Collectors Invite You to Browse." *Gentleman's Quarterly* 58, no. 1 (January 1988): 154–59. Contains a picture of Kennedy's study and his comments about his love of books.

Moritz, Charles, ed. "William Kennedy." In *Current Biography Yearbook, 1985.* New York: H. W. Wilson Company, 1985. 223–36. General but informative biographical and literary information.

Nichols, Loxley F. "William Kennedy Comes of Age." *National Review* 37 (9 August 1985): 46–48. Places Kennedy's novels in literary perspective.

Prescott, Peter S. and Susan Agrest. "Having the Time of His Life." *Newsweek* 103 (6 February 1984): 78–79. Additional biographical facts and literary insights into Kennedy's life and career.

Rachlis, Kit. "It's About Time, Part I: Kennedy and the Week That Was." *The Boston Phoenix,* 24 May 1983, 1–2. Valuable for Kennedy's comments and article's information about Viking's editors.

————. "It's About Time, Part II: Kennedy and the Years That Were." *The Boston Phoenix,* 31 May 1983, 2–3. Valuable for Kennedy's comments and article's information about his literary career.

Reilly, Edward C. "Dante's *Purgatorio* and Kennedy's *Ironweed:* Journeys to Redemption." *Notes on Contemporary Literature* 17, no 3 (May 1987): 5–8. Draws interesting parallels between the two works and their redemptive themes.

————. "The Pigeons and Circular Flight in Kennedy's *Ironweed*." *Notes on Contemporary Literature* 16, no. 1 (March 1986): 8. Uses Jake Becker's pigeons in novel's closing scenes to prove that Francis Phelan returns home.

————. "William Kennedy's Albany Trilogy: Cutting through the Sludge." *Publications of the Arkansas Philological Association* 12, no. 1 (Spring 1986): 43–55. An analysis of Kennedy's heroes: Legs Diamond, Billy Phelan, and Francis Phelan as they struggle to put purpose and meaning in their lives.

Robertson, Michael. "The Reporter as Novelist: The Case of William Kennedy." *Columbia Journalism Review* 24 (January–February 1986): 49–50, 52. Contains biographical information and insights into Kennedy's journalism and literary career.

Ryan, Michael. "The Making of *Ironweed*." *People Weekly* 29 (18 January 1988): 84–87. A general, glitzy article about stars of the film; not the same information found in McNamee's "The Making of *Ironweed*."

"Shot Twice Before: Diamond Bodyguard by Turns for 'Little Augie' and Rothstein." *New York Times,* 27 April 1931, 13. Interesting article for determining how and what facts Kennedy translates into fiction.

Tarshis, Lauren. "Afterword." In Claudio Edinger's *The Making of Ironweed.* New York: Penguin Books, 1988. Informative and candid insights by and about Babenco, Kennedy, and others involved in making the film.

Weaver, Warren. "Daniel P. O'Connell Is Dead at 91: Old Time Albany Political Boss." *New York Times,* 1 March 1977, 34. Complements Kennedy's essays in *O Albany!* and McCall's characterization in *Billy Phelan.*

Whittaker, Stephen. "The Lawyer as Narrator in William Kennedy's *Legs.*" *Legal Studies Forum* 9, no. 2 (1985): 157–64. Interesting analysis of Marcus Gorman's role in *Legs.*

Index

About the Author

After receiving his B.S. and M.A. degrees from Memphis State University and teaching at Christian Brothers High School and in the Memphis school system, Edward C. Reilly joined the English Department at Arkansas State University. He completed his Ph.D. at the University of Mississippi in May 1989. His published work includes articles on William Kennedy, John Cheever, John Irving, Jim Harrison, John Kennedy Toole, E. L. Doctorow, and Ken Kesey, and he is completing a book about John Irving for the University of South Carolina Press. His "A William Kennedy Bibliography" will appear in *Bulletin of Bibliography*, 1991.

The Editor

Frank Day is a professor of English at Clemson University. He is the author of *Sir William Empson: An Annotated Bibliography* and *Arthur Koestler: A Guide to Research.* He was a Fulbright Lecturer in American Literature in Romania (1980–81) and in Bangladesh (1986–87).